THE
JERSEY RAILWAY
(J.R. & T.)

by
N. R. P. Bonsor

THE OAKWOOD PRESS

© Oakwood Press 1962

First Published September 1962
Reprinted with additions June 1969
.Second reprint 1986

ISBN 0 85361 344 3

Printed by S & S Press, Abingdon, Oxford

*To
Christopher
(Captain E. C. Lance, D.S.O.)
in memory of
the happy afternoons
we spent in search
of railway remains*

Published by
THE OAKWOOD PRESS
P.O. Box 122,
Headington, Oxford

AUTHOR'S NOTE

In this short history I have endeavoured to unfold the story of the Jersey Railways & Tramways Co. Ltd., and its predecessors in such a way as to attract not only the specialist reader, whoever or wherever he may be, but also to interest the general reader and particularly the Jersey resident, whether or not he or she remembers the old days of railway travel in the Island.

It has not been an easy task to select and arrange the subject matter, of which I have been fortunate in amassing a vast quantity. I dare hardly hope to please all my readers all the time, but feel confident that everyone will find a good deal of interesting material. If some parts appear to have little appeal the best plan will be to skip them!

Many people have been most helpful. First and foremost, I must thank the Directors of the Jersey Motor Transport Company Limited, and in particular Mr. E. S. Leach, the General Manager, and Mr. J. E. Le Couteur, the Secretary, for so kindly letting me have access to the J.R. &T. minute books, annual reports and balance sheets from 1896 onwards. They have made a tremendous difference to the completeness of the story. Thanks are also due to Mr. J. F. Yeates and Mr. R. Falle of the Jersey Public Library for placing at my disposal the countless bound volumes of the "British Press & Jersey Times", "Chronique de Jersey", "Evening Post", "Morning News" and "Nouvelle Chronique de Jersey" and also for much assistance; to Mr. V. Boyd-Carpenter, a director of Edward Exley Ltd., Baslow, Derbyshire, for permission to include his notes on the special trains run for the German prisoners and also the details of engine and carriage rotas, etc.; to Mr. G. Bird and Mr. R. G. Burt, author of "The Old Jersey Railways", for information and a number of photographs; to Mr. M. Ginns and Mr. J. Slade for valuable information that will appear in Volume II regarding the German Occupation Railways and to Mr. L. P. Sinel, author of the "Occupation Diary", for permission to quote extracts therefrom. Others to whom I would express my warm thanks in a number of ways are:—Mr. E. Bisson (late J.R. &T.); Mr. S. W. Bisson (Judicial Greffe); Mr. M. Deane; Mr. E. F. Guiton (Société Jersiaise); Mr. S. A. Holley (States Greffe); Mr. G. B. Johnson; Mr. G. C. H. Le Cocq (Société Jersiaise); Mr. C.

Le Fol (late J.R. & T.) and Mrs. Le Fol; Mr. H. Marie (late J.E.R. and late J.R. & T.); Mr. P. Marsouin; Mr. E. P. Pead; Mr. J. Tardivel (late J.R. & T. and now of the J.M.T.); Mr. J. C. Vincent and Mr. R. E. B. Voisin. Also to the North British Locomotive Company Limited and the editor of "Engineering".

I should be very interested to hear from readers who are in possession of further information or photographs.

N. R. P. Bonsor.

"Brookside",
Petit Port,
Corbiere,
Jersey, C.I.
1962.

The Island of Jersey

JERSEY, the largest of the Channel Islands, has an area of 45 square miles, measuring about 10 miles from east to west and six from north to south. The population is 63,000—some 8,000 more than 100 years ago. Nearly 50 per cent of the inhabitants live in St. Helier which, contrary to what is still said in some guide books, has always been the island capital.

During the early years of the 10th century the Channel Islands became part of the Duchy of Normandy, and the fact that Duke William of Normandy defeated King Harold of England at the battle of Hastings (1066 and all that!) and became King William I of England enables the Jerseyman (and doubtless the Guernseyman, too) to claim with his tongue in his cheek, but with a certain amount of justification that his island conquered England.

Jersey remained under the jurisdiction of the Duchy of Normandy until 1204, when King John was driven out of France, and has ever since owed allegiance to the sovereigns of England except during seven years of occupation by the French in the 15th century and five years by the Germans during World War II. The Jerseyman is proud of his British nationality and the fact that his Island is one of the British Isles, although it is not part of the United Kingdom. Jersey is, perhaps, best described as a self-governing Dominion, although technically it does not come within this category and is, in fact, an "appanage of the Crown". The jurisdiction of the Island Parliament does not extend to the other principal islands—Guernsey, Alderney and Sark.

Some details of the Island's administration will help in studying the chequered history of its railways. The representative of the Crown in Jersey is the Lieutenant-Governor. The head of the Island Government is the Bailiff, who is appointed by the Crown and presides over the Royal Court, which consists in addition of 12 Jurats (Magistrates). He is also President (Speaker) of the Island Parliament, which is known as the "States of Jersey" or more commonly "The States"

and is composed of 12 Senators (elected for a term of nine years), 28
Deputies (elected for three years) and the Constables (Mayors) of
each of the 12 Parishes. In addition, the Attorney-General, the Solicitor-
General and the Dean represent the Crown and have a voice in the
States but no vote. Bills passed by the States become law upon confirmation by Her Majesty in Council, but certain short-validity Acts
can be passed without sanction.

   The official language of Jersey is French and many of the official
documents such as Bills (*Projets de Loi*), pleas and conveyancing
contracts are still drawn up in that language, although there is a
growing body of opinion in favour of replacing French by English
as far as is practicable. Apart from certain introductory formalities, the
proceedings of the States are conducted in English, which practically
every permanent resident in the Island is able to speak fluently. Jersey-
French, often referred to as the local patois but which is in reality the
old Norman language, is still commonly heard in country districts.

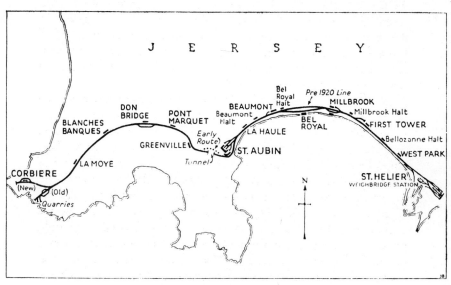

The Jersey Railway (not to scale)

The Jersey Railway

IT would appear that the inhabitants of Jersey first began to discuss the possibility of having a railway within a very few years of the beginning of regular rail travel in the United Kingdom. The French language newspaper *Chronique de Jersey* of 5 July 1845 referred to a prospectus published in the London newspapers for the formation of a railway company and the building of a new harbour in Jersey. The capital was to be £300,000 and the names of the Jersey directors were given as Messrs. Jean Le Couteur (*Viscount*), François Bertram, Clement Hemery, Dr. Macreight, Messrs. Edouard Nicolle Jr., Nicolas Le Quesne, David De Quetteville and James Robin.

A well-patronised meeting was held in St. Helier on 8 October 1845 to hear the report of the directors of the new concern, known as the Jersey Railway Company, and to meet a delegation of five men described as deputies of the London directors. Mr. Jean Le Couteur, in the chair, opened the proceedings by saying that at one time he had had serious doubts about the success of the enterprise, but he was now convinced that it would be advantageous to the Island, and that he would give the scheme his support.

Mr. Fripp, the head of the English delegation, pointed out that the railway would start at St. Aubin and terminate beside the sea at St. Catherine's. He admitted that they might meet certain difficulties with the Ordnance Office concerning the exact location of the line, but did not think that there would be any serious obstacle. The cost of construction had been estimated at £10,000 a mile. He was unable to say exactly how much the harbour would cost, but if one allowed £100,000, that would bring the total to £250,000. He assessed the total population at 50,000, and as the railway would pass through eight parishes he thought that the revenue would be sufficient to pay a dividend of 6 or 7 per cent. In England during the previous year railway profits had amounted to £7,000,000. If the Island's population spent eight shillings per head per annum on the railway and if 20,000 visitors did the same that would produce an annual income of £28,600. He also said that the railway would be valuable for the defence of the Island in wartime. Further, he drew attention to the fact that ships would be able to enter and leave the harbour in St. Catherine's Bay at all states of the tide, and that it would be possible to travel from Jersey to London in the fast time of eight hours if the steamers proceeded direct to an English port.

Mr. Edouard Nicolle, Senr. said that he did not wish to place any obstacles in the way of the project, but he believed that many of those who had asked for shares had since refused them, and that if the scheme depended upon Island support nothing would come of it. He declared that he would use all his influence as an individual and as a member of the States to make the scheme succeed. (Applause.)

Mr. P. R. Lemprière was against the scheme, and Mr. François Godfray said that if the truth were known, the shares were probably valuable only as waste paper; the prospectus contained untruths and was full of deception of the worst kind. (Sensation!) The Jersey gentlemen whose names had appeared as directors had considered it desirable to write to the secretary to have them removed. Mr. Viscount Le Couteur was chairman without having any directors. Who had nominated him to the position? And as for what one found in the prospectus concerning the extension of the line to St. Brelade's Bay and St. Ouen's Bay, it must have been written about some place other than Jersey, for one was well aware that traffic in these bays was never unusually large but was, on the contrary, unusually small. The meeting broke up at 7 p.m. without a decision.

The *Jersey News* of 11 October 1845 contained a well-reasoned editorial on the subject of the railway. It pointed out that at the lowest estimate the cost would be £10,000 a mile, and that the two termini plus locomotives and rolling stock would cost another £10,000. The obvious thing was to examine the prospects for that part of the line offering the most promise—namely, between St. Aubin and St. Helier, a distance of about four miles, for which the cost would be about £40,000 plus the additional £10,000 already mentioned, making a total of £50,000. To this must be added £7,000 to cover interest of 14 per cent promised by the directors and another £2,000 to £3,000 per annum to cover working costs. The article went on to say that according to reliable information the total takings of the omnibuses running between the two towns were not more than £1,300 per annum, and even supposing this revenue were doubled there would not be a penny piece to pay interest on the capital. As regards other parts of the Island, the loss would be even greater. It had been proposed to extend the railway to St. Brelade's and this would probably cost about £20,000 per mile—simply and solely to capture the handful of passengers who travelled to town by omnibus! But even worse was the extravagant proposal to build a tunnel under Fort Regent. The project was completely absurd! The deficit on the line to St. Catherine's would also be very great because the company would have to buy the land at a high cost.

In 1847 the Admiralty arranged for work to start on St. Catherine's breakwater. The real reason behind the move was that relations between Britain and France were very strained because of the marriages of Queen Isabella of Spain and of her sister, Louisa—hence the desire to build a harbour, capable of sheltering a large British fleet, as close as possible to the French coast. It is highly probable that the choice of St. Catherine's Bay was influenced by the railway activities just described. Work continued for several years, but although a sum of about £250,000 was spent, only one arm of the breakwater was ever completed. A temporary contractor's railway was used in connection with the works.

It may be of interest to add that a two mile length of standard gauge permanent way was laid, at about the time that work started in St. Catherine's Bay, in the neighbouring island of Alderney, to carry granite from two quarries to Alderney harbour breakwater, then under construction by the Admiralty. This line is still in existence and is the sole surviving railway in the Channel Islands.

A Second Unsuccessful Attempt

More than a decade elapsed before any further attempt was made to start a railway in Jersey. In fact, it was not until November 1860 that it was announced that the local directors of what was described as the

"St. Helier & St. Aubin's Railway Company" were Messrs. Ph. Le Gallais, Joseph Dickson, John De Caen, Elias De Carteret and Geo. Benest. On 15 January 1861 a railway bill consisting of 59 articles was read to the States of Jersey and lodged "*au Greffe*". That is to say, the Greffier of the States was instructed to have the bill printed and distributed to members for further consideration on a date to be arranged.

The matter came again before the States on 7 February, when a committee was appointed to prepare a bill, hear objections and examine the plans already lodged. One of the members of the committee was Jurat De Quetteville who, as Mr. David De Quetteville, had been present at the 1845 meeting, and whose name will crop up again on a number of occasions.

On 11 September 1862 the bill, by then extended to 68 articles, was adopted by the States subject to certain modifications, and finally, on 22 January 1863, it was decided that the bill should be sent for confirmation by Her Majesty (Queen Victoria) in Council. The company was described as the "Jersey Railway Company, Limited", the title mentioned previously being only an indication of the towns between which it would run.

The capital was stated to be £25,000, with permission for an increase in capital of up to £6,000 subject to agreement at a General Meeting. The railway was to be built in conformity with plans approved by the States. It might consist of a single line or of more than one set of rails. The service was to be carried out by means of steam locomotives. No mention was made of the gauge to be adopted.

Article 46 made provision for access to shipyards along the route— whether already existing or built at some future date, and No. 47 allowed the company to take possession of all the seashore below the high water mark of spring tides, also including the following: "The Company will not be required to pay for this concession any indemnity either to Her Majesty or to the States of this Island".

Article 55 stipulated that in the event of disagreement over any property situated within the limits indicated on the plans, the claimant should not cause work to cease by raising the *Clameur de Haro*.*

* See Appendix

The complaint should be lodged with the Royal Court for consideration and decision as soon as possible.

Article 56 fixed a maximum fare of 6*d.* single, first class, or 9*d.* for return on the same day; and 4*d.* single, second class, or 6*d.* for return on the same day, between St. Helier and St. Aubin; and No. 60 laid down that there should be a minimum of six services a day in each direction between St. Helier and St. Aubin. If the company failed to provide a full service during 60 or more days in the course of a year—except on Sundays, or when the line was out of action owing to necessary repairs, or unless permission had been granted by the Main Roads Committee—the company would be considered to have abandoned the enterprise and the States would be empowered to take possession of the railway, without compensation. Article 64 empowered the States at any time they thought fit to purchase the railway by repaying the capital plus 33½ (*sic!*) per cent.

Although the bill had taken two years to reach this stage, one would have been justified in hoping that only routine formalities remained. Not so! In the opinion of Mr. Clarke, a well-known local shipbuilder, whose yard was roughly opposite what is now known as West Park, the railway would interfere seriously with his activities, in spite of the protection afforded by article 46. A petition was accordingly sent to the States, who appointed a committee under the chairmanship of Jurat De Quetteville to study the contents, which reported on 6 March 1863 that it did not come within the province of the States to consider the petition, and concluded by praying Her Majesty in Council not to postpone giving her sanction to the railway bill.

That Her Majesty in Council did postpone sanction—but apparently not for this particular reason—will be evident from the fact that the records of the States show no further mention of the railway until 28 April 1869, more than six years later, when the President informed the House that he had received a letter from the Lieutenant-Governor, containing a despatch from the Lords of the Treasury regarding an objection against the 47th clause of the Railway Bill passed in 1862. At a meeting held to consider the Government's objections, on a remark respecting the Treasury, Jurat De Quetteville said: "Oh! We must put a stop to the perpetual intervention of that Department. We must have nothing to do with it". It is evident that correspondence had been passing between the authorities in England and Jersey during the years 1863-69 but it is difficult to find an adequate explanation or justification for the long delay.

The Building of the Line

After some further delay, a new Bill in the name of the Jersey Railway Company, Limited, was passed by the States of Jersey on 22 October 1869 and was confirmed by Her Majesty in Council only 20 days later. In general, the details were very similar to those of the unsuccessful Bill of 1863, but the sentence objected to in Article 47 was omitted. On the other hand, the articles dealing with the *Clameur de Haro*, maximum fares, frequency of services, right of the States to purchase the railway, etc., remained unchanged, but the time allowed for starting construction was reduced from twelve months to three and for completing the line from three years to one. An entirely new Article was rightly inserted at the end to the effect that the railway was not to be opened to the public until a certificate was produced by an engineer appointed by the States that the works had been satisfactorily carried out in accordance with the Law and with due regard to the safety of the public. Further, the Main Roads Committee was empowered at all times to order the line to be inspected by a competent person of its choice, and to suspend all operations until work necessary for public safety had been carried out. There was a slight reduction in share capital from £25,000 to £24,000. It is evident that the contractor, Mr. E. Pickering, had put up the greater part of the capital.

One of the difficulties of building the line was that from West Park onwards—that is to say, for over 3 miles of the total of 3¾ miles from St. Helier to St. Aubin—no sea wall existed at that time, and as the railway was planned to run very close to the high-water line there was a decided risk of the track being washed away during bad weather. On 16 December 1869 the States considered a communication from Mr. Pickering offering to build a sea wall from Mr. Clarke's shipbuilding yard at West Park to St. Aubin. The matter was referred to the

Committee of Defence, who reported that Mr. Pickering had undertaken to build the wall at a cost of £30,000, and to fill in a space of
90 feet from the face of the wall, of which 30 feet would be for the use
of the railway and 60 feet for a carriage-way and promenade. It was
also proposed that the States should agree to the removal of part of the
slaughter-houses to make way for the St. Helier terminus. Although
the railway company stipulated for two years to complete the sea wall,
this would not prevent them from completing the railway for public
use during the ensuing season.

The plans for the construction of the sea wall were approved by
the States on 11 March 1870, and 12 days later Jurat De Quetteville
read the report of the Defence Committee and the Harbour Committee, approving Mr. Pickering's plans and suggestions concerning
the slaughter-houses and for acquiring certain public property on the
Esplanade. Soon afterwards the Jersey public began to realise for the
first time that if the proposals were carried out in their existing form
the railway would run on the sea side of the Esplanade, greatly to
the detriment of anyone wishing to take a stroll along the front. A
petition was accordingly placed before the States and the matter
resolved to everyone's satisfaction by Mr. Pickering agreeing to leave
room for a six foot wide pedestrian promenade adjacent to the sea.

The States were hastily summoned on 30 May 1870, when the
Bailiff announced that a member, Jurat De Quetteville, had raised the
Clameur de Haro with regard to the demolition of the slaughter-houses
on the Esplanade. Jurat De Quetteville then addressed the States
asserting that when the Act of 6 April was passed authorising Mr.
Pickering to run the railway along the Esplanade, the legislative body
was unaware that the project would involve the demolition of the
slaughter-houses to the extent carried out by Mr. Pickering. The only
method of stopping him had been by raising the *Clameur de Haro*,
which he did on the previous Saturday, 28 May, as he considered that
a question of public interest was involved. The Attorney-General
maintained that Mr. Pickering's action had been sanctioned and could
not be mistaken, nor could its nature be misconstrued. A motion to
maintain the Act of 6 April having been rejected, and a counter-
motion by Jurat De Quetteville carried by a majority of three, further

demolition of the slaughter-houses was forbidden until the difficulties had been ironed out.

Following the appearance of a letter from Mr. Pickering in the *British Press & Jersey Times* of 1 June 1870, ventilating the whole matter, the States met again on 20 June and passed a resolution to the effect that the States had authorised Mr. Pickering to continue his work on condition that he allowed the butchers access to the slaughter-houses now standing, and the question as to the locality of the buildings remained deferred. A fortnight later a newspaper paragraph stated that the railway was making steady progress and that "undoubtedly the opening would have taken place before now had not the unfortunate *Clameur de Haro* been raised for no purpose—unless indeed to hinder the progress of the works in hand".

Few constructional details have been discovered before the following 22 June, when the attention of newspaper readers was drawn to a wooden structure at First Tower, stated to be the temporary station of that name.

On 24 August mention was made that on the two previous days a great many people had been to the St. Helier terminus to inspect three carriages which had been built locally. They were described as being very elegant, constructed according to the most recent design and, being open, would be all the more suitable for summer use.

On 10 September it was stated that no date had been fixed for the opening of the line, but that the works were officially said to be in a state of completion. Mention was also made of the fact that the locomotive and winter carriages were expected almost daily.

The screw steamer *Dublin* from Liverpool arrived in St. Helier's roads on the 23rd, and during the afternoon moored alongside the quay at the top end of the Albert Pier, being one of the largest steamers that had entered the harbour for some time. Her cargo included four closed carriages for winter use, three of them being carried side-by-side on deck. It was stated that "the carriages are all composite ones. Two of them are break (*sic!*) vans". A likely explanation of this rather contradictory statement is that two carriages were "brake seconds" and the remaining two "first and second class composites". In addition the *Dublin* carried two locomotives, one in one hold and one in another, and a great many people watched all six items being hoisted on to the quay by the crane, which had been moved to the appropriate spot for the purpose.

The Opening of the Line

During the afternoon of 28 September 1870 everything was ready for the trial trip of the first of the engines. "After a slight difficulty had been at first felt and overcome in the setting of it in motion, it steamed from off the siding of the station up to the junction of the main line, on which it returned into the station." At 5-45 p.m. the engine started off for St. Aubin in the presence of hundreds of spectators. Besides the driver and fireman it had on board Mr. E. Pickering (the contractor), Mr. W. H. Le Feuvre (the chairman), Mr. J. C. Craven (the consulting engineer) and "a favoured half-dozen". No attempt was made to test the running powers of the engine; the trip to St. Aubin and back was made without incident.

On the following day, a special train consisting of the engine and four open carriages stood in St. Helier station in readiness to take a party of about 300 invited guests on a trial trip to St. Aubin and back, and by 3 o'clock the carriages were filled by many of the principal businessmen of the town and not a few members of the States. Wrote a local journalist:

"Already the steam whistle of the engine had sent forth its shrill voice, when some commotion among the passengers was caused by the appearance of Mr. Jurat De Quetteville. The effect was really startling and made itself universally felt. He was received with acclamation on all sides, which finally lapsed into a general roar of laughter as the worthy member of the legislative chambers of Jersey took his place in the railway compartment, almost over the very spot where *jadis* he raised the notorious *Clameur de Haro*. Finally at six minutes past three o'clock, the various members of the cortege began to tremble and the whole machine was in motion. The cheers that rang from the mouths of the numerous groups of persons lining the Esplanade were loud and prolonged; and the only doubt as to the success of the trip was the fear (?) expressed by one gentleman that the Jersey Constitution, so numerously represented, might be shattered at a blow and occasion the advent of a new régime. Nothing of the kind, however, occurred, and the journey to St. Aubin's pretty station, which was decorated with flags for the reception of the visitors, was accomplished in 17 minutes. Not a little amusement was caused when the train, slackening its speed before entering the station of St. Aubin's, gradually overtook and passed the omnibus: Prince Jehu thereupon strained his utmost nerve to prevail, but failed in his endeavours to do so, amid the derisive laughter of those who rode the better horse. Almost immediately after the train arrived at St. Aubin's it returned with rather more than half its complement to the pretty spot of the bay in the vicinity of La Haule, and a photograph *in extenso* was taken on the spot." (This photograph is reproduced on another page.)

The train returned from St. Aubin's at 4-17 p.m. and calling intermediately at Beaumont and Millbrook, completed the journey in 22 minutes including stoppages. As on the previous day, Mr. J. C. Craven was in charge. This "tough, ruthless, grim-faced person" (to quote Mr. Hamilton Ellis) had been Locomotive Superintendent of the London, Brighton & South Coast Railway from 1847 until the end of 1869.

Further trial trips were made, that on 8 October carrying 180 invited passengers in some of the closed carriages.

The States met on 13 October, when the Bailiff announced that the line was complete and ready for an official examination by an engineer appointed by the States. The Constable of St. Mary asked how it was that the Act of the States relative to the grant of £30,000 to Mr. Pickering for building a sea wall and the permanent line had not been confirmed by Her Majesty in Council. Jurat De Quetteville stated that the Committee of which he was the chairman had communicated with the Home Government to ascertain whether the *Impôt* for the term of 18 years could not be allowed by the Government. The reply was that unless the States followed the recommendations submitted to them by the Government on a former occasion they did not feel

Société Jersiaise

The first train on the Jersey Railway, at La Haule four weeks before the opening of the line in 1870. Engine 'Haro Haro' and open carriages with verandahs

Farewell gathering for Mr. R. Carnegie, the manager, in 1883. Locomotives 'Duke of Normandy' and 'Haro Haro'

Jersey Motor Transport Ltd.

'Duke of Normandy' at St. Helier. Note the old station roof, and that the locomotive is facing the opposite way to that of the picture on the previous page

P. Marscuin

Converting the line at St. Aubin from standard to narrow gauge in 1884. Note 'Haro Haro's' cab.

St. Helier terminus before the erection of the office building in 1901. Note the old roof similar to that at St. Aubin

St. Helier terminus as altered, showing office building and new roof

No. 4, 'St. Brelades' at St. Helier, showing station roof built about 1900

Miss Dickson
No. 2 proceeding along flooded track near West Park in 1913

No. 4 at West Park in 1896, soon after it was placed in service

Société Jersiaise

The only known photograph of one of the narrow gauge 0–4–2 saddle tanks built for the St. Aubin's & La Moye Railway in 1877. At First Tower between 1885 and (probably) 1893

R. F. Smith

No. 2, 'St. Aubyns', at First Tower in 1928. For many years this was the spare locomotive

E. Bisson

Millbrook station in the 1930's. The building survives as a tea room

La Haule station, whose corrugated iron waiting room became a beach kiosk and was removed in 1968 owing to road widening

No. 1 'St. Heliers', at St. Aubin in 1912, showing the old station roof. Note vacuum brake pipe on locomotive; carriages lighted by electricity

No. 3, 'Corbiere', before rebuilding in 1911, at the Corbiere platform at St. Aubin. Note carriages lighted by oil

G. Bird

No. 1, 'St. Heliers', before rebuilding in 1910, with mixed train at La Moye (Note spelling La Moie)

G. Bird

No. 1 near La Moye with train of early carriages

St. Aubin's station before removal of the old roof R. G. Burt

St. Aubin's tunnel, cut through solid rock in 1898 to do away with a series of reverse curves

R. G. Burt

St. Aubin's station showing umbrella roofs built in 1922

inclined to do anything with regard to the *Impôt*. After there had been some further remarks, the Bailiff recommended the States to proceed with the nomination of a competent engineer in confirmity with the law. Jurat De Quetteville then proposed the appointment of Mr. J. C. Craven, and also that his certificate that the line was ready for opening to the public should be sufficient to answer the requirements of the provisional railway until the will of Her Majesty was known regarding the permanent line. The line was inspected by Mr. Craven on 17 October.

During the afternoon of the 15th a train consisting of three carriages had made a non-stop journey from St. Helier to St. Aubin in 7 minutes, the time taken for the return being 7½ minutes. Amongst the passengers were several members of the States and Mr. Parson, the chairman of the Metropolitan Railway (London).

It was announced on 22 October that the receipts for the first three days would be given to the fund for the building of a new church at St. Aubin's. The following advertisement appeared in the *British Press and Jersey Times*:—

JERSEY RAILWAY COMPANY LIMITED

INAUGURATION OF THE RAILWAY FROM ST. HELIER
TO ST. AUBIN

The Railway will be opened for Public Traffic on Tuesday, the 25th instant.

A special train will leave St. Helier at 1 o'clock to convey the guests of the company to St. Aubin.

Afterwards trains will run for the accommodation of the public as follows:—
From St. Helier to St. Aubin at 2, 3, 4, 5, 6, 7, 8 and 9 o'clock.
From St. Aubin to St. Helier at 1-30, 2-30, 3-30, 4-30, 6-30, 7-30, 8-30 and 9-30 o'clock.

None of the above trains will stop at the intermediate stations.

Fares:—					1st class	2nd class
From St. Helier to St. Aubin ..	..	..	..	..	6*d.*	4*d.*
From St. Helier to St. Aubin and back	..	..	..	9*d.*	6*d.*
From St. Aubin to St. Helier ..	..	..	..	..	6*d.*	4*d.*
From St. Aubin to St. Helier and back	..	..	..	9*d.*	6*d.*

British currency, but Jersey coppers will be taken and given.

By Order   PH. LE NEVEU, *Traffic Manager*,
4 Esplanade, Oct. 21. 1870.

The Lieutenant-Governor of Jersey, Major-General P. M. N. Guy, arrived at the St. Helier terminus at a few minutes before 1 p.m. on 25 October 1870 and was received by a guard of honour of the Rifle Company of the Town Battalion. After the customary inspection, he declared the railway to be formally opened, his words being greeted by a discharge of 13 guns by a battery of the Royal Jersey Artillery. The special train, containing His Excellency and the Bailiff and about 180 of the principal inhabitants of the Island, consisted of four coaches and was drawn by the locomotives *Haro Haro* (in the lead) and *Duke of Normandy*, the former being, of course, so named after the *Clameur de Haro* which Jurat De Quetteville had raised some five months previously. The train left punctually at 1 o'clock.

A guard of honour of a Company of the South West Regiment of Militia was drawn up at St. Aubin, and after it had been inspected, the Very Rev. the Dean delivered an eloquent address, in which he commented on the wonderful powers of steam; prayers for the Divine blessing of the undertaking followed. The guests then took their seats in horse carriages and drove to Noirmont Manor, the residence of Mr. Pickering, the contractor, where "a *déjeûner* of the most sumptuous character was partaken of". A long list of toasts followed, the principal speakers being Mr. W. H. Le Feuvre, the chairman of the company, who presided, the Lieutenant-Governor and the Bailiff. The chairman said that he had asked Mr. Pickering to reply for the company and had been informed that he would rather build another railway than make a speech.

The speeches were not concluded until 6 o'clock, whereas it would appear that the special train back to town was scheduled to leave St. Aubin at 5-30 p.m. We are not told what alternative arrangements were made, but the railway company must have come up against their first traffic problem. The line was well-patronised throughout the afternoon and evening, the receipts amounting to £60, which suggests that a total of over 4,000 single journeys was made.

The entrances to the St. Helier terminus faced the weighbridge; it was intended to erect "a façade of great beauty" but, in fact, a delay of over 30 years occurred before this was done. There was one platform only—on the Conway-street side—that is to say, on the side furthest from the harbour. The line was single and ran in a gentle curve round St. Aubin's Bay, the total length being approximately 3¾ miles. After proceeding along the Esplanade for about a quarter of a mile it continued along the sea shore on level ground except for a short distance at and beyond La Haule, where it was raised on wooden piles. St. Aubin's station had two platforms. There were intermediate stations at First Tower, Millbrook and Beaumont, each being supplied with a booking office. Although a detailed contemporary report made no mention of this, it seems clear that Millbrook station had a crossing loop from the first, but the second platform may have been added later.

Early Activities

There was a strong wind and an exceptionally high tide during the evening of 26 October 1870, and it was discovered the following morning that the railway had sustained slight damage near Beaumont and near the People's Park. A gang of labourers set to work and the 11-10 a.m. and subsequent trains were able to run as scheduled. The railway was being quite well patronised, and in the afternoon of the following day a train from St. Helier to St. Aubin carried nearly 100 passengers, whilst on the Saturday morning two trains each brought between 60 and 70 passengers into St. Helier. On the first Sunday after opening more than 3,000 passengers were carried, and on the following Sunday the total was 3,726, the receipts being £48. 6. 1. On this occasion a half-hourly service was being run during the afternoon, this necessitating the use of two trains, which passed each other at Millbrook. As from 12 November, the company arranged for horse omnibuses to meet incoming trains at St. Helier and convey passengers to points in the town as far as the "Robin Hood", Springfield, at a fare of 1d. Parcels were delivered at the station for ½d. each.

The railway opened an hotel at the St. Aubin terminus in May 1871. A bar was accessible direct from the platform; above it was a spacious balcony with a saloon and coffee rooms upstairs. It was announced that a band would play three times a week. To begin with the place was well-patronised and certainly attracted a lot of extra traffic for the railway; on the second Saturday after opening it was stated that the railway carried over 9,000 passengers.

In June 1871 a third engine arrived in the Island and was placed in service on the 18th of that month. It was described as being several horse-power more powerful than the other two.

Among the events of 1872 was the opening, on 14 February, of new stations named Cheapside and People's Park. The former was opposite the Hotel Victoria-Eugénie, which was on the site of the present Grand Hotel. Many years later this station was renamed Westmount and later still West Park. The station at People's Park was situated approximately half way between Cheapside and First Tower. It attracted but little traffic and was closed five months later, on 20 July. Soon afterwards the station building was moved to Goose Green and became part of a new station named Bel Royal. It was claimed that this would be very suitable for people living in the parishes of St. Peter, St. Mary and St. Lawrence. At that time fares from St. Helier to Bel Royal or Beaumont were the same as to St. Aubin. Not very long afterwards a station was opened at La Haule, thereby making the total number of intermediate stations six, namely:—Cheapside, First Tower, Millbrook, Bel Royal, Beaumont and La Haule.

During the early morning of 1 March 1873 a strong wind combined with a spring tide did serious damage to the line at both Millbrook and Beaumont, and at the latter the rails sank by as much as three feet. All traffic was suspended for four days and passengers had to proceed by omnibus between St. Helier and St. Aubin "though this mode of conveyance is not so acceptable as it formerly was". On 5 March a test train consisting of two locomotives, two passenger carriages loaded with rails, and eight waggons loaded with ballast, the total weight being over 100 tons, was run from St. Helier to Bel Royal, and that section of the line was certified as fit to be reopened to traffic. Trains recommenced running to St. Aubin on 11 March.

The traffic receipts from 25 October to 31 December 1870 were £1,205, for the whole of 1871 £7,409, for 1872 £6,566 and from 1 January to 31 March 1873 £1,000, making a total of £16,190. The average per annum was £6,476, of which one-half, namely

£3,238, was stated to be absorbed by working expenses. Of the remaining £3,238, repairs and renewals to the line, including groins, culverts, etc., accounted for £850, leaving a balance of £2,388. Allowing £600 for interest on the £12,000 worth of debentures and £1,680 for interest on the preference share capital of £28,000, the nett balance was £108, which was carried forward, but would have been just sufficient to pay 5 per cent interest on the Ordinary capital of £2,000. In 1870 95,000 passengers were carried, in 1871 597,000 and in 1872 517,000.

It was announced at the Annual General Meeting on 3 May 1873 that the directors proposed to abandon the Bill for the construction of a sea wall, as they were of the opinion that this would entail a heavy loss to the company. They considered that an extension of the existing groins and culverts, and the construction of some new ones would be just as satisfactory. The eventual outcome was that the Committee of Defence took the building of a wall in hand, and by 1880 it had been completed for about half the distance from West Park to First Tower, and work on the second half was due to start. The total cost of these two sections exceeded £20,000 for a distance of less than three quarters of a mile, whereas Mr. Pickering had estimated a sum of £30,000 for over three miles. It is sad to relate that only a few weeks later bankruptcy proceedings were started against him, so it seems probable that other enterprises of his had been similarly underpriced.

In view of the passing of the dividend, it was up to the company to devise means of increasing traffic. The company had applied to the States for permission to lay tramways on the piers, so that it would be able to ballast ships for considerably less than it then cost, and at the same time make a handsome profit. The company had lost money on the hotel at St. Aubin and the refreshment rooms at St. Helier and had let these out.

The chairman at a meeting on 11 August 1873 mentioned that a turntable and an "engine house" had been built out of revenue. An element of mystery surrounds the question of the turntable as no trace has been found of one having existed at either St. Helier or St. Aubin, and obviously a turntable at one end of the line would have been of little or no use without one at the other. In any event, there was no apparent need for a turntable at all as tank engines can run bunker first without difficulty. However it seems clear that the Jersey Eastern Railway had a turntable at Green Street and their need of one was no greater and no less that that of the Jersey Railway, so we must take the chairman's word that one was provided. It will be relevant to add that at a later date, after the change of gauge to 3 ft. 6 ins. it was invariably the custom for the engines to run chimney first from St. Helier to St. Aubin and Corbiere because it is well-known that this helped them slightly in the ascent of the steep gradients beyond St. Aubin and ensured that the firebox was covered with water. However, before the opening of the Corbiere extension it seems that there was no uniformity in the direction that the engines faced and this may well have been due to the occasional use of a turntable.

It is not generally known that the Jersey Railway Company, Limited was declared *en désastre* as early as December 1874—when it had only been in operation for a little more than four years. The Viscount reported to the Royal Court on 8 May 1875 that it would be to the advantage of all parties that the rolling stock should not be sold to different persons, as it would be of use to those who made themselves *tenants*. On the application of the Attorney-General, the Court ruled that the line should, for the benefit of the public, be kept open to traffic during the *décret*.

The final meeting of the creditors and debenture holders was held before the Greffier on 17 July 1875 when, according to custom, various persons having claims against the railway company were asked personally, or through their proxies, whether they would accept the tenantship. Several persons renounced their claims, but finally Mr. Louis Marie was adjudicated proprietor of the railway. He entered into possession of the line on 24 July 1875.

In lighter vein, trains between St. Helier and St. Aubin were delayed on 19 and 20 January 1875 by a ship lying across the line near First Tower. It was being launched by Messrs. Deslandes & Le Sueur, whose yard lay on the inland side of the railway, thereby making it necessary for the vessel to cross the line. By some defect in the launching the ship stuck fast when on the railway and traffic was necessarily suspended. The company was unable, in a literal sense, to get round the difficulty, but they overcame it to a considerable extent by running one train up to the obstruction, and requesting the passengers to walk to a train waiting on the other side of the vessel.

The *British Press & Jersey Times* of 14 September 1875 reported that owing to a temporary disablement of the engine *Haro Haro*, the 10-15 p.m. train on the previous evening from St. Helier to St. Aubin was unable to run as the other two engines were both undergoing repairs. Season ticket holders and those with return tickets were conveyed to the various destinations in road vehicles.

Following some remarks in the States regarding the safety of the line, the entire track from St. Helier to St. Aubin was inspected on 31 March 1876 by Mr. P. H. Le Sueur, the States' architect, and Mr. C. S. Le Cornu, the company's engineer. Three months later, on 17 July trains ceased to run beyond La Haule in order that repairs to the wooden "viaduct" could be effected. This continued until 23 September 1876, when the 7 p.m. train stopped at La Haule to set down all the passengers and then in order to test the line proceeded on to St. Aubin. This test having proved satisfactory, the 8 o'clock train proceeded through to St. Aubin at a slow pace with its passengers on board.

In view of the fact that the railway was originally intended to be a temporary makeshift until a sea wall was built from West Park to St. Aubin, the intermediate stations were not of a very substantial nature. It was announced in September 1877 that the trains had recently been obliged to use the "outer siding" at Millbrook while the wooden platform was being replaced by a "solid wall foundation, the pathway covered with gravel, and the line and station raised". Similar improvements had already been introduced at Cheapside and First Tower and were undertaken, soon afterwards, at Beaumont.

Early in 1876 there was a project on foot to introduce a steam tramway in St. Helier to connect the termini of the Jersey Railway and the Jersey Eastern Railway, and to serve the upper part of the town. It was proposed to work the line on the same principle as the Guernsey Steam Tramway, which was then under construction. Nothing came of the scheme, nor of a subsequent proposal in October 1879 for a tramway to proceed along the main road from St. Helier to St. Aubin. In fact, the petition lodged *au Greffe* was for a horse tramway, but as one of the clauses contained an undertaking not to use steam without the consent of the Main Roads Committee, it is evident that the eventual use of steam power was contemplated.

Whilst on the subject of tramways it may be of interest to mention that a much more elaborate scheme came before the States in February 1882—from Grouville via Grouville Hill, Longueville, Don Road, Royal Crescent, Colomberie, Esplanade, St. Aubin's Road, Beaumont, Beaumont Hill, St. Peter's Church and St. Ouen's Manor to a terminus at the top of L'Etacq Hill. This was also unsuccessful.

In February 1878 Mr. Louis Marie transferred his rights to Mr. F. Nalder for a consideration believed to have been about £15,000. The latter in turn rented the line to Mr. Alexander Gopsell Pooley, and in September 1879 the Metropolitan Bank obtained an order that he should give up possession of the railway to the receiver and manager appointed by the Court. In October 1879 Mr. Pooley was adjudicated bankrupt and soon afterwards left England. In May 1880 the trustee in bankruptcy obtained permission to prosecute him for offences against the bankruptcy laws and he was accordingly arrested in Paris under the Extradition Act, tried and acquitted. However, while he was still in Newgate prison the Metropolitan Bank obtained an order that when released from the criminal charge he should be handed over to the Governor of Holloway prison for contempt of court, in that he had not given possession of the railway to the receiver, as instructed. Mr. Pooley was released in May 1881 after he had executed a power of attorney vesting in the trustee or the receiver all his interest, whatever it was, in the Jersey Railway.

The manager appointed by the Court in September 1879 was Mr. Rodney Pooley, presumably a relative. When, in March 1881, Mr. Frederick Nalder sued Mr. A. G. Pooley for certain arrears of rent, as he could not pay, he had to give up possession of the line. Mr. Rodney Pooley vacated the post of manager. The following copy of a testimonial dated 18 March 1881 indicates that the railway was being run efficiently and that Mr. Pooley had been on excellent terms with the travelling public:—

To Rodney Pooley Esq., late manager of the Jersey Railway.

Sir,

We, the undersigned season-ticket holders and others, have learnt with much regret that you have ceased to be the manager of the Jersey Railway.

During the time it has been under your management no accident has occurred.

On certain holidays such as the Queen's Birthday, or when there have been public entertainments at St. Aubin's, when the capacities of the line were taxed to the utmost, not only have all the passengers travelled in safety and comfort through your quiet and steady care, but at all times the same care and attention have been paid by you for the safety, comfort and convenience of all.

The skilful and expeditious manner in which, under your direction, the line has been repaired when high tides and winds have on different occasions crippled it, must not pass without a word of praise.

We are, dear Sir,

Your sincere friends and well-wishers,

(Here followed a list of signatures)

Whether Mr. Frederick Nalder himself took over the management is not known, but it is evident that relations between the new manager, whoever he was, and the travelling public were somewhat strained. In a letter to the *British Press and Jersey Times* of 12 August 1882, Vice-Admiral T. Saumarez wrote: "Nothing is done towards the convenience of the passengers beyond incivility from the manager when complaints are made".

On this rather bitter note we must leave the Jersey Railway Company, Limited.

North Western Railway Company, Limited

Within a few months of the opening of the Jersey Railway on 25 October 1870, the first steps were taken to promote two more lines, namely, the Jersey Eastern Railway, which is dealt with in a second Volume, and the St. Aubin's & La Moye Railway & Granite Quarries Company, Limited. This was not completed for well over 10 years and, in consequence, it will be convenient to deal first with a third line. On 6 January 1872, less than a year after the other two newcomers had been first heard of, an advertisement in French appeared in the *Chronique de Jersey*, the following being a translation:—

NORTH WESTERN RAILWAY COMPANY

At a meeting of the promoters of this railway, held at St. Aubin on January 2nd, 1872, the following resolutions were adopted:—

(1). A public meeting will be called to take into consideration the construction of the proposed railway for the benefit of the parishes of St. Brelade, St. Peter, St. Ouen, St. Mary and St. John. This meeting will be held in the Parish Hall of St. Peter on Monday next, 8th January, 1872, at 6-30 p.m.

(2). Committees will be nominated in the parishes of St. Brelade, St. Peter, St. Ouen and St. Mary to further this project, and will meet at the Royal Yacht Club Hotel on Saturday (today), 6th January, at 2-30 p.m.

(3). For the furtherance of this project, a Bill will be presented before the States during the next session.

(4). Ph. Payn Esq., (in the event of his being elected Deputy of St. Ouen) being fully prepared to propose, and Jurat Le Montais to second the Bill in the States, the matter will be placed in their hands.

> W. H. Le Feuvre (*President*)
> Rev. G. W. Clement
> T. Le Cornu
> Ph. D'Auvergne
> Ph. Le Feuvre (La Hougue)
> Jurat Le Montais
> Ph. Payn
> and others

On 10 January 1872 the same newspaper announced that at a further meeting the company was unanimously named the North

Western Railway Company, Limited. Several people present signed
the subscription list, which totalled £2,000, and the route that the
railway would take was approved. It was arranged to hold a further
meeting. Mr. W. H. Le Feuvre was also, as has been seen, chairman
of the Jersey Railway.

Although it was announced on 31 January 1872 that the Bill
was ready to be presented to the States, no further information is
available about the North Western Railway until almost exactly a
year later, when it was proposed and carried unanimously that the
railway Bill should not be lodged at that time owing to the difficulty
of coming to terms with the St. Aubin's & La Moye Railway. On
the other hand it was stated that landowners in the north-western
parishes had expressed their willingness to subscribe the necessary
capital to construct the line, and that plans were being prepared for
the construction of tramways from the terminus of the Jersey Railway
in St. Helier to the new harbour; these would be of great advantage
to the North Western for developing goods and granite traffic. It was
decided at the meeting to make a small call on the shares to meet
current expenses.

This is the last mention that has been found of the North Western
Railway, as such, and reading between the lines it would seem that
the difficulty in coming to terms with the St. Aubin's & La Moye
Railway was due to the fact that this company wanted to build their
own branch to St. Peter. At their meetings in June and August 1873
hopes were expressed that an extension to St. Peter would be authorised. Further, at the general meeting of the Jersey Railway in March
1874 Mr. H. F. Barnett, the St. Aubin's & La Moye Company's
solicitor, was invited to address the members present and after mention-
ing the difficulties that his company was experiencing, expressed the
opinion that once these were overcome their line would be completed
between St. Aubin and La Moye, and that it would be extended from
the vicinity of General Don's farm to St. Peter's Church and subsequently to St. Peter's Mill. Moreover it was pointed out that this
would be the only railway reaching the tableland of the Island and
would be able to serve such places of interest as Grève-de-Lecq.

Hitherto, very few people seem to have heard of the North

Western Railway, but it is fairly well known that the name *North Western* was chosen for a 2-4-0 tank built in 1871-72. A likely explanation will be found in due course.

Don Farm to St. Peter's Church Railway

As already stated, nothing was heard of the North Western Railway after 1873, and it will be seen shortly that the St. Aubin's & La Moye Railway was never completed as such. Work on it remained in abeyance from 1877 until 1883, when it was acquired by a new concern known as the Jersey Railways Company, Limited, who went ahead energetically with its construction.

Although not in strict chronological sequence, it will be convenient to mention at this stage that the inhabitants of the parish of St. Peter seem to have been extremely keen to have their own railway. The *Chronique de Jersey* of 26 January 1884 under the heading *Chemin de Fer de la Ferme Don à l'Eglise de St. Pierre* (Don Farm to St. Peter's Church Railway), stated that at a meeting on 23 January a committee was formed to interview the owners of the land through which the projected line would pass. The intention was undoubtedly for the line to connect at Don Farm (or as we know it, Don Bridge) with the St. Helier—St. Aubin—Corbiere line of Jersey Railways.

The line in question was never built, but the Germans completed a branch from Pont Marquet to Ronez on a course that for part of the distance ran roughly parallel with the projected Don Farm to St. Peter's Church Railway. We must regretfully leave this concern with the observation that as likely as not its title was the most picturesque and unsophisticated one ever chosen for a full-size railway.

St. Aubin's & La Moye Railway & Granite Quarries Company, Limited

On 15 March 1871 the Constable of St. Brelade presented a petition to the States on behalf of Mr. Maxwell Bury, the owner of the granite quarry at La Moye, that they should allow him to construct a tramway from La Moye to St. Aubin, whence granite and other goods would continue via the Jersey Railway to St. Helier for shipment.

The Bill for the St. Aubin's & La Moye Railway & Granite Quarries Company, Limited, was passed by the States on 7 June 1871. The capital of the company was £25,000, the company was allowed a period of two years from the date of registering the Order in Council to complete the line and put the service into operation, the maximum charge for passengers between St. Aubin and La Moye was not to exceed 2*d.* a mile or fraction of a mile first class and 1½*d.* a mile or fraction of a mile second class; there were to be a minimum of three departures daily from St. Aubin to La Moye and *vice versa*. A clause prohibiting the raising of the *Clameur de Haro* was inserted as before.

At a general meeting of the company held on 22 March 1873 the chairman, Mr. R. W. Johnson, Deputy-Lieutenant of Worcestershire, stated that the works would start shortly. In the meanwhile the company's engineer, Mr. J. G. McKenzie, was busily engaged in setting out the line; they contemplated erecting a pier at St. Aubin to facilitate the shipment of granite and other materials, and thus avoid the extra cost of transit over the Jersey Railway.

However, at an extraordinary general meeting on 27 June the chairman, reported that the whole of the line had been resurveyed. Some of the landowners were asking sums far beyond the utmost value; one near St. Aubin asked more than £400 an acre for a piece of rock of no apparent value and completely unproductive. He added that he doubted very much the advisability of continuing, and was inclined to recommend the shareholders to abandon the undertaking altogether. The proposition was carried that the directors be authorised after further efforts to continue or abandon the scheme, as they thought best.

Perhaps the chairman's remarks served as a warning to the land profiteers, for it was announced on 11 August that building operations had started that day near General Don's farm (situated at what is now known as Don Bridge).* Two-thirds of the land had already been purchased, within a week operations would be in progress in three different places and the railway would probably be opened for traffic within six to nine months. It would carry an extensive goods traffic as well as passengers and it was estimated that a minimum of 50,000 tons of granite a year would be carried from La Moye quarry alone. In addition it had been discovered that there was a much larger quantity of china clay in the vicinity of the line than was at first realised. A depot for vraic (seaweed) near General Don's farm was also proposed.

The company's solicitor asked the States on 25 March 1874 for four things: an extension of time, an increase in capital, a deviation from the proposed line and approval of previous deviations. A Bill consisting of 10 articles and providing for deviation, an increase in capital from £25,000 to £35,000, settlement by arbitration of any difficulties which might arise and an extension of two years from the date of registration of the Bill in the time granted for the completion of the works, was passed on 3 September. Mr. W. H. Le Feuvre, the chairman of the Jersey Railway, addressed the House with respect to the running powers granted to the St. Aubin's & La Moye Railway over the Jersey Railway and pointed out that this would entail heavy expense and necessitate two booking offices and a double set of clerks. He also stressed the importance of a uniform gauge, without which the Mainland "battle of the gauges" might be renewed in Jersey on a small scale.

At the annual general meeting of the St. Aubin's & La Moye Railway on 6 June 1874 the chairman had stated that after so much trouble and delay they were determined to go on with the enterprise. Since August of the previous year the contractors had pushed on the works with much vigour. An interesting point brought out at the meeting was that it had originally been intended that the railway, for a short distance, should leave St. Aubin along the road known as Mont-les-Vaux—that is to say, along the main road to St. Brelade's

* Lieut-General Sir George Don was Lieutenant-Governor of Jersey from 1806 to 1814, and was responsible for the construction of many of the Island's roads.

Bay and La Moye—but that this would no longer be allowed. After careful consideration, and on the advice of their engineer, they had decided on a new route at an increased cost, likely to be as much as £7,000.

It was stated on 1 March 1875 that rapid progress was being made in the construction of the line, and that a portion of the road, near Seven Oaks, from St. Aubin to St. Brelade's Bay had been cut through to a depth of about 30 feet to enable the erection of an arch to carry the road over the railway. This was completed about three months later and the road was re-opened to traffic.

During the early part of 1876 the company was declared *en désastre* and all work ceased until 9 May, when Mr. William Lyster Holt made arrangements for it to be resumed; on 29 July 1876 he was confirmed as *ténant après décret*. Three months later temporary rails had been laid as far as Seven Oaks and there was much activity at the rear of the water mill at St. Aubin, where some houses were being demolished and large quantities of rock shifted.

By December 1876 temporary rails had been laid from the water mill in the direction of the Jersey Railway Company's terminus to enable rock from the excavations to be dumped in the hollow between the station and the harbour. In the middle of January 1877 the sailing ship *Sea Bird*, of Jersey, discharged rails, fishplates and spikes at St. Aubin's harbour and the lugger *Francis* delivered a large quantity of sleepers.

A further suspension of work took place in March 1877, but the arrival of the brig *Jeune Marie* on 13 May with another cargo of sleepers coincided with a general resumption of work under the auspices of Mr. Horace Henry Holt, who had taken over the ownership of the company.

By the end of July rails extended from St. Aubin to Pont Marquet, laid to a gauge of 3ft 6ins. There is little or no doubt that the original intention was to build the line to the "standard" gauge of 4ft 8½ins. It is not certain when the decision was reached to change to 3ft 6ins. gauge; however, the reason is perfectly clear: the succession of extremely sharp curves between St. Aubin and Pont Marquet and probably also the steep gradients. Mention was made of the fact that the Jersey Railway track would have to be fitted with an "interior rail" before through running to and from St. Helier would be possible. The archway at Seven Oaks had been completed and presented "a very sightly appearance, having been faced with worked granite", and progress was being made in St. Aubin's market, a portion of which had been placed at the company's disposal.

The first of the two engines, the *General Don*, was being assembled in an engine shed built at the rear of Mr. Le Brun's stores at St. Aubin and made its first trial trip on 10 September 1877, when it steamed as far as Greenville, after which it went backwards and forwards several times, testing the line.

> The *British Press & Jersey Times* stated on 4 December 1877: "The town of St. Aubin's has lately been thrown into considerable confusion owing to the works of demolition and reconstruction carried on by the St. Aubin's & La Moye Railway. No little ill-feeling has been raised by the manner in which the operations have been undertaken. Everything has had to give way to this new line, much to the inconvenience of the public generally. The worst part at present is the level at which it has crossed the foot of Market Hill and the Quay, which causes no small inconvenience to ordinary traffic."

A surprising development ocurred only a few days later, on 22 December, when, with the exception of a few masons, all the men working on the railway were discharged. The masons were retained temporarily to complete Don Bridge, which was designed to carry the main road from St. Peter to St. Brelade's Bay over the railway, as until this was opened for traffic there would remain a gap in the road about 20 feet in width and about the same in depth.

The suspension of work on the line can be regarded as the final phase in the story of the St. Aubin's & La Moye Railway, as such. In July 1878 a *désastre* was declared on the property of Mr. Horace Henry Holt, and Mr. Thomas Hayward Budd, being a heavy creditor, became *ténant après décret*. He took no steps until January 1882 to obtain possession of the two locomotives, which had been held in custody by the Viscount; the Royal Court then ruled that he could take them over provided he defrayed the expenses incurred.

The Completion to La Moye and Change of Gauge

Behind the scenes, apparently, there was still some activity, for there appeared on 20 February 1883 an advertisement in the *British Press & Jersey Times* in respect of the issue of £60,000 5 per cent Perpetual First Mortgage Stock of the Jersey Railways Company, Limited (note the plural). The directors were given as Mr. J. W. H. Williams (Chairman), who was also a director of the Rathkeale & Newcastle Junction Railway Company; Mr. A. C. Jones of Jersey; Mr. H. A. Cowper, a director of the Donna Theresa Christina Railway Company of Cuba; and the Hon. Dudley Murray of London. The trustees were the Right Hon. Viscount Ranelagh, K.C.B., and Mr. E. B. De Fonblanque. The prospectus stated that the trustees would retain in their hands such portion of the proceeds as might be required for completing the railway, under the contract which had been entered into with Messrs. James Perry & Co., of London, the contractors, and would only disburse this against the resolution of the board on the certificate of the company's engineers, Sir Charles Fox & Sons, thus ensuring the completion of the entire system within the time fixed by the contract.

It was stated that the then net receipts of the first section already opened alone amounted to £2,079 per annum, and that the net receipts of the entire system, when completed, were estimated at £7,989, whereas the total debenture interest only amounted to £3,000 per annum.

The Rector of St. Mary drew the attention of the States to this prospectus, and to the fact that the company wished to borrow from the public the sum of £60,000 under the guarantee of the concession granted by the States to the St. Aubin's & La Moye Railway Company in 1871 and 1874. On examination of the law he had found that these concessions had been granted for a specified time, which had lapsed, and he therefore proposed that the Committees of the States be authorised to take possession of the land which reverted to the States. The proposal was lodged *au Greffe*.

Mention has already been made of the fact that in 1878, Mr. Thomas Hayward Budd became *ténant après décret* of the St. Aubin's

& La Moye Railway Company Limited. On 22 March 1883 Deputy Durell presented a petition to the States on Mr. Budd's behalf to the effect that he was the proprietor of the land of the partly-constructed railway to La Moye and that he had made arrangements to purchase the line from St. Helier to St. Aubin, but was not in any way connected with the Jersey Railways Company, Limited, and had nothing to do with the prospectus issued by that company; that the time allowed for the construction of the La Moye Railway had expired, the reason why it had not been completed being lack of capital and the impossibility of amalgamating with the Jersey Railway Company owing to continued lawsuits in England; further, that since the expiration of the concession he had been compelled by the States' Committee to undertake certain costly works in St. Aubin's market, and that in so doing it was respectfully submitted that he had preserved the concession. All obstacles to the completion of the line had been resolved, and if the States thought fit to renew the concession, the lines of the Jersey Railway Company Limited and of the St. Aubin's & La Moye Company would be transferred to a new concern known as the Jersey Railways Company, Limited, provided a sum of £60,000 could be raised.

At the meeting of the States on 5 June 1883, the Greffier read the report of the joint Committees of Markets, Main Roads and Harbours, which had been instructed to examine the works on the projected line between St. Aubin's and La Moye. Deputy Durell stated that much of the opposition against the Bill to permit the completion of the line seemed to have been caused by the false idea that £60,000 had been borrowed in connection with the La Moye Railway. This was not the case. This line only formed one section of the whole, the reconstruction of the St. Helier—St. Aubin line and the purchase of new rolling stock being responsible for the greater part of the total. The La Moye section only represented about £18,000 to £20,000. The Bill was adopted with slight alterations, caution money of £1,500 being imposed.

Mr. Budd did not in fact purchase the Jersey Railway Company Limited as apparently he had at the time intended to do, and on 17 July 1883 he sold his interest in the St. Aubin's and La Moye Company to Viscount Ranelagh and others, who purchased the Jersey Railway Company Limited on the same date from Mr. Frederick Nalder. The Jersey Railways Company Limited was duly established to control both the St. Helier—St. Aubin and the St. Aubin—La Moye lines. It was an English company, with a registered office in London. Mr. Budd was appointed chairman.

Two months later it was announced that work on the extension beyond St. Aubin was proceeding rapidly and that 50 men were in full-time employment there. The *Chronique de Jersey* of 19 March 1884 gave the interesting information that the first trial trip had been made on the 15th, that the carriage was decorated with flags and flowers and that Lady Marett, the wife of the Bailiff, and her family were passengers, the Bailiff himself being absent for health reasons. Others present included Mr. P. P. Guiton, one of the directors, and Mr. Torr, the manager.

It has already been indicated that the La Moye line had been laid to the 3 ft. 6 ins. gauge, and that the *General Don* and another engine had arrived in the island by September 1877. It seems clear that one or other of these engines drew the special train; the passenger carriage referred to must have been specially built locally, or converted from standard gauge, or had arrived recently in the island.

The s.s. *Camel* arrived in St. Helier harbour from Liverpool on 30 March 1884—a fortnight after the trial trip—bringing with her two large locomotives for use on the line from St. Helier to La Moye. It was stated that they would be named *St. Helier* and *St. Aubin* respectively,* and that they appeared to be the most powerful locomotives ever brought to the Island. Ten new carriages and three brakevans had also been purchased; the extensive alterations in the line were gradually approaching completion.

The *Nouvelle Chronique de Jersey* of 24 February 1884 stated that for several days past a large gang of men had been relaying the

---

* In fact the exact spelling adopted was "St. Heliers" and "St. Aubyns". This was incorrect and they should have been either "St. Helier's" and "St. Aubin's" (with an apostrophe) or, preferably, "St. Helier" and "St. Aubin". For the past 200 years the accepted spelling of St. Aubin has been with an "i" and not a "y".

line between St. Helier and St. Aubin, and mentioned that the old rails had not been attached to one another at all rigidly, with the result that there had been excessive wear near the joints, thereby causing discomfort to the passengers. Work must have started about the middle of February in converting the St. Helier—St. Aubin line to 3 ft. 6 ins. gauge, and a press report makes it clear that the first section to be taken in hand was that between St. Aubin and Bel Royal, and that this was completed by or before the end of April. Passengers from St. Helier to St. Aubin had to alight from the train at First Tower, whence they were transported in horse-drawn carriages. It seems that they rejoined the railway at Bel Royal and then travelled in the "new carriages" to Beaumont, La Haule and St. Aubin; these were described as being very comfortable, with seats facing one another and running from one end of the carriage to the other, like the old-fashioned omnibus, instead of having several compartments, as formerly. As they were undoubtedly of 3 ft. 6 ins. gauge, this confirms that the section from St. Aubin to Bel Royal had already been converted. It is also clear that by 26 April 1884 steps were being taken to convert to narrow gauge the section between First Tower and Bel Royal.

At the annual general meeting of the company on 15 December 1885, the chairman, Mr. T. Hayward Budd, in reviewing the results of the 12 months starting on 10 July 1884, mentioned that for $2\frac{1}{2}$ months of the period takings had been seriously reduced by the fact that the line was being relaid; expenses had been unusually heavy as passengers had had to be conveyed in omnibuses over the part affected. From this one is justified in inferring that the change of gauge was not completed until the end of September 1884. As work had started in the previous February one cannot help thinking that it had progressed very slowly, bearing in mind that the distance between St. Helier and St. Aubin is under four miles. Part of the delay was undoubtedly due to the non-arrival of the new rails from England, which at one stage had caused the States to intervene and threaten closure.

On 25 July 1884 the Greffier read the report of Mr. H. G. Hammond Spencer, the engineer of the Jersey Eastern Railway, who had been engaged to inspect the St. Aubin—La Moye line. It stated that as an important alteration had still to be made in the lower section of the line, it was proposed to start the service from a temporary terminus near St. Aubin's Hospital (*sic!*)—that is to say, from a point about 100 yards to the west of what in 1898 became the western end of a newly-built tunnel. The report gave details of the sharp curves that had to negotiated, and stated that the gradient up to Don Bridge averaged 1 in 40. Brake power was of the utmost importance as, should the carriages become detached from the engine when ascending the bank they would, unless they had exceptional brake power, run down the incline at a very dangerous speed. Two brakes were essential; heavy brake vans were required, with brake power to all wheels, the brake power at present provided being insufficient for actual traffic. Speed from Don Bridge to St. Aubin should not exceed 10 miles an hour, and the maximum speed near the old main road should be five miles an hour. With these improvements, the line might be opened for traffic from St. Aubin's Hospital to La Moye Quarries.

On 29 August 1884 the Main Roads Committee announced that it had authorised the new line to be opened from St. Aubin to Corbiere (i.e. La Moye Quarries) and the following advertisement appeared simultaneously:—

JERSEY RAILWAYS COMPANY, LIMITED

LA MOIE SECTION

On and after Saturday, 30th August, the trains will run on weekdays as follows:—

From St. Aubin	*From Corbiere*
11-30 a.m.	12 noon
2-45 p.m.	3-10 p.m.
3-30 p.m.	5-00 p.m.
6-30 p.m.	7-00 p.m.

On Sundays

9-30 a.m.	10-05 a.m.
2-45 p.m.	3-05 p.m.
3-30 p.m.	4-40 p.m.

John Fraser, *Manager.*

Mention has already been made of the first trial trip over the line, but no trace has been found of any official opening ceremony. In fact, one of the few scraps of information available at about this time is that the 2-45 p.m. train from St. Aubin to Corbiere on Sunday, 31 August

1884 carried no fewer than 300 passengers. As there was no physical connection with the St. Helier—St. Aubin line it seems certain that this train was hauled by the *General Don* or the companion locomotive.

From the temporary terminus near St. Aubin's Hospital the line took a winding course "upwards through a beautiful glen, giving alternate glimpses of precipitous rocks, green hollows, romantic cottages, slopes covered with fern and ivy, and broad expanses of furze and heather". Principal engineering works were an overbridge at Seven Oaks carrying the main road from St. Aubin's to St. Brelade's Bay and Corbiere, an underbridge near Greenville and an overbridge named Don Bridge. There were intermediate stations at Greenville, Don Bridge (within reasonable walking distance of St. Peter's Barracks in one direction and St. Brelade's Bay in the other) and La Moye,* the terminus at Corbiere being then situated a few yards short of La Moye quarries. The line was single throughout except for a short passing loop at Don Bridge where, however, there was only one platform, as was also the case at the other stations. There was a run-around loop at Corbiere. Within a few years an additional station was opened at Pont Marquet, half-way between Greenville and Don Bridge, and later still one at Blanches Banques, for La Moye golf course.

Many hundreds of tons of rock had to be blasted and removed before the junction of the two lines could be completed at St. Aubin. Work proceeded steadily, but it was not until 5 August 1885, nearly a year after the Corbiere opening, that the first through train ran from St. Helier to Corbiere.

On weekdays there were six through trains from St. Helier to Corbiere and five in the opposite direction, and three in each direction on Sundays. In addition, there were 13 weekday trains from St. Helier to St. Aubin and 14 in the opposite direction, with 11 each way on Sundays. A special through platform had been built at St. Aubin's terminus for Corbiere line trains.

Four new carriages arrived by the s.s. *William* from Bristol on 12 July 1887 and were landed on the Albert Pier. Unlike the

* A photograph shows that the station name was spelt La Moie. The official name of the earlier railway was spelt "MOYE". In fact, both spellings are used in the locality.

remainder of the rolling stock they were of the ordinary compartment type instead of having longitudinal seating, the builders being the Bristol Wagon Works Company. Hopes were expressed that "the complaints as to jolting will soon cease".

As has already been seen more than once, the line between St. Helier and St. Aubin was very vulnerable to wind and tide, particularly the spring tides of the March equinox. Another occasion when a serious interruption took place was on 30 March 1888. A considerable gang of men spent the day clearing the line between Bel Royal and La Haule, trains running between St. Helier and Bel Royal only, a fleet of omnibuses and covered carriages being in waiting there to convey passengers to St. Aubin. It was stated that it was not possible to meet the demand for seats on these conveyances, and in consequence the journey from St. Helier to St. Aubin took as long as an hour and a half. It would have been quicker to walk!

The affairs of the Jersey Railways Company Limited, turned out to be every bit as complicated as those of its predecessor. Following the death of Viscount Ranelagh in 1886, Mr. De Fonblanque decided that he would like to retire from the trust and on 4 June 1888 Messrs. F. W. Lowther, T. Hayward Budd and H. A. Whitaker were appointed. Three months later a certain John Fraser purchased for £23,000 the shares held by Messrs. De Fonblanque and Lowther, and on the following day resold them for a similar sum to the three trustees, the apparent reason for this manoeuvre being that one trustee could not make a direct purchase of another trustee's shares. On 25 January 1889 the trustees sued the Jersey Railways Company Limited in the High Court of Justice, Chancery Division, and the Court appointed Mr. Edward Cecil Moore as receiver and manager.

In March 1893 Mr. T. Hayward Budd abandoned his interests in the railway to Messrs. Lowther and Whitaker for £7,666 13. 4.— that is to say, for one-third of the price the three together had originally paid—and in May of the same year he was released from the trusteeship. During the same month, Mr. W. H. Dickson, of St. Peter, Jersey, took up the post of manager. The first evidence of his determination to adapt the service to meet the requirements of the public ocurred on Whit Monday 1893, when a series of excursion trains ran to Corbiere, return fares being 10*d.* second class from St. Helier and 6*d.* from St. Aubin.

The two engines *St. Heliers* and *St. Aubyns* had been mainly responsible for carrying on the service as a whole ever since the line was opened throughout in 1885, although it is believed that the two saddle tanks of 1877 vintage assisted from time to time. Even so, the company was undoubtedly in need of additional motive power. and on 18 July 1893 the 2-4-0 tank locomotive No. 3 *Corbiere*, which had arrived in the Island a few days previously, made its first trial. After proceeding "light" to Corbiere, it returned to St. Aubin, whence it proceeded with three carriages and two brake vans as far as Greenville, "the curves on that part of the line being admirably rounded".

The company celebrated its 25th anniversary on 25 October 1895 and in honour of the occasion the engines were gaily decorated with flags. It was stated that a dinner was to be given to the employees at the then new "Corbiere Pavilion", and that a train would leave St. Helier after the arrival of the last train, stopping at all stations en route to pick up the staff. "The festivities will, we hear, be kept up until the small hours of the morning." No further information is available, so presumably the homeward train eventually got back safely to town!

This 25th anniversary was not really an opportune moment for rejoicing as, only four days later, it was decided at an extraordinary general meeting that the company could no longer continue in business and that it would be expedient to place it in voluntary liquidation. Mr. E. C. Moore was appointed liquidator. On 17 December 1895 a conditional agreement was made between the liquidator and Messrs. W. H. Venables Vernon, Clement Le Sueur and E. H. Bayldon, who had formed a syndicate to purchase the business subject to the sanction of the Court of Chancery. The necessary permission was granted on 7 January 1896.

It is evident that the original prospectus of the Jersey Railways Company Limited had greatly overestimated the company's earning capabilities. In fact, on two occasions only was the total annual revenue substantially higher than the estimated net profit of £7,989; on three occasions it was virtually the same and on no fewer than six occasions it was less.

Jersey Railways & Tramways Limited

The Jersey Railways & Tramways Limited (J. R. & T.) was registered on 18 January 1896 by Messrs. W. H. Venables Vernon, Clement Le Sueur and E. H. Bayldon with an ordinary capital of £30,000 which was augmented a few days later by £24,000 worth of 4½ per cent mortgage debentures. The new company took over the assets of the Jersey Railways Company Limited as from 1 February 1896, the price paid, including concessions, freehold and leasehold lands and buildings, rolling stock, plant and machinery being £53,881 18. 2.

Mr. Vernon was appointed chairman, his fellow directors being Messrs. E. H. Bayldon, C. Le Sueur, E. C. Moore and Colonel E. S. Walcott. The post of manager was occupied by Mr. W. H. Dickson, who had occupied a similar position with the predecessor company for the previous three years.

The first event of interest in the life of the new concern was the arrival at St. Helier on 29 January 1896 of locomotive No. 4 *St. Brelades (sic!)*, which was placed in service a few days later and was exactly similar to its immediate predecessor. It had, of course, been ordered well before the new concern came into being.

Plans for several important new developments were formulated in quick succession, the first being a new station building at St. Helier. Others were a new station and refreshment room at what had originally been called "Cheapside", was then known as "Westmount" and was to be renamed "West Park"; a new station between West Park and First Tower to be known as "Bellozanne"; and enquiries were to be made about the acquisition of land on the right-hand side of the road leading from La Moye quarries to Corbiere, with a view to the extension of the railway. In addition, permission was given for rails to be laid from the level crossing opposite Castle Street to the first steps leading into the Albert Pier. The board decided to put this matter in hand as quickly as possible, but the West Park and Bellozanne developments were indefinitely postponed.

The first annual general meeting of the company, held on 16 February 1897, was auspicious as it was decided in addition to paying the interest on the debentures to declare a dividend of 3 per cent on the ordinary shares, this being, so far as is known, the first occasion in the history of the railway that the ordinary shareholders received any return on their money. Resolutions were passed that, following the report of Messrs. Vernon and Dickson, who had visited various electrical systems both at home and abroad, a Bill should be promoted for powers to use electricity either in addition to or in substitution for steam on the the section of line between St. Helier and St. Aubin (the Bill for the extension line did not stipulate motive power), and to enable the line to be extended from the terminus near La Moye quarries to a new one in the grounds of the Corbiere Pavilion.

Nothing further was heard of a tramway scheme which had been discussed at a board meeting held on 29 October 1896 and which, if the title of the company be anything to go by, had at one time loomed large in the minds of the founders of the company.

In May 1897 an early train for the benefit of workmen was scheduled to leave St. Helier at 6-15 a.m. for St. Aubin and Corbiere. It returned from Corbiere at 6-53 a.m. and St. Aubin at 7-10 a.m. and was known as the "boat train", being due at St. Helier at 7-27 a.m., in plenty of time for the outgoing London & South Western Railway and Great Western Railway steamers to Southampton and Weymouth respectively. A further convenience was that a van met the train at the town terminus to convey luggage to the boats. On the day following the announcement of these trains there was a serious landslip at St. Aubin, the line between St. Aubin and Corbiere being blocked from the early morning of 6 May 1897 until 7-30 p.m. on the following day.

It was decided in July 1897 to cut a tunnel through a piece of land recently acquired by the company from the heirs of Mr. T. Hayward Budd, who in 1883 had become the proprietor of the Jersey Railway Company Limited. The site was a few hundred yards to the west of St. Aubin station, the object being to straighten the line and do away with a severe curve. The tunnel was opened to traffic on 26 December 1898.

In March 1898 the board requested Mr. Dickson to survey a suggested line, in tunnel, from Greenville to St. Brelade's Bay, and report back to them. No further minute on the subject has been discovered.

Mention has been made of the sea wall running from St. Helier to First Tower and of the fact that this was nearing completion by 1880. There was a long pause before a further section was started, but on 30 September 1898 Mr. Dickson reported to the board that he had arranged for material for the back of the new wall between First Tower and Millbrook. In May 1900 the States requested the company to shift the track between First Tower and Millbrook to a position in closer proximity to the sea in order to make room for the extension of Victoria Avenue.

At the third annual general meeting on 23 February 1899, the new chairman, Colonel Snowdon Robin, referred to the resignation of his predecessor, Mr. W. H. V. Vernon, from the chair and the board on account of his appointment to the office of Bailiff. A resolution was passed that the capital of the company should be increased to £50,000 by the issue of £20,000 worth of cumulative preference shares. For the third year running a dividend of 3 per cent was declared on the ordinary shares.

The Corbiere extension was officially inspected by the States' Engineer on 22 June and opened to the public on 1 July 1899. It was decided simultaneously to close Greenville station "as the traffic to and from that station does not warrant the expense incurred in stopping heavy trains on such a steep incline, and the time thus saved is also required to run the extra mileage opened at the Corbiere".

The New Station Buildings at St. Helier

The new station buildings at St. Helier were completed and opened in 1901. They included new offices for the company, a board room, refreshment rooms and two rooms on the ground floor suitable for shops or offices, the total cost being approximately £2,500. In February 1902 the manager was instructed to fix a "traversing and slewing table" in the station at a cost not to exceed £50. This traverser was described as follows in the *Model Engineer & Electrician* of 8 October 1914:—

"The amount of traffic throughout the year does not warrant the expense of having an engine kept waiting for the purpose of hauling out a train. It means, therefore, that the engine bringing in the train must of necessity take it out. In the ordinary course of events the train is not composed of many carriages, and the engine is consequently able to stop the train well down the platform, be uncoupled, steam down to the buffers, and be shunted on to the loop line, whence it is an easy matter to be brought to the front of the train. During the holiday season, however, when passenger traffic is heavy, this procedure would entail a considerable amount of inconvenience to both the public and the railway officials. To overcome the difficulty a happy idea in the form of a moving track has been instituted. That portion of the line immediately in front of the buffers, of sufficient length to accommodate an engine, is cut away from the main track and placed on wheels, which in turn run on guides. There are eight wheels of the solid type to each rail, four being placed on either side. When the engine is ready for transposition the moveable portion is unbolted from the main track and a porter energetically turns the handle affixed to the big wheel. Through bevel gearing the horizontal bar below the wheel is made to revolve, and, working through the windlasses at both of its extremeties, hauls in the rope attached to the nearer rail, the other end of the rope being affixed to the other rail after passing under the line and over a pulley on the platform side. When the moveable track has been pulled flush with the adjoining line the engine proceeds in the usual way, the wheel is reversed, and the rail is once more brought into communication with the main track."

The traverser did not replace the run-around loop, which was still used when the length of the train so permitted.

In January 1903 the manager was authorised to spend £250 in fitting automatic vacuum brakes to two engines, four carriages and two brake vans. After extensive trials, instructions were given for the other two engines and two additional carriages to be similarly fitted, and for the remainder of the carriages and brake vans to be piped throughout; this work had been completed by March 1904. *The Locomotive* of 15 January 1914 reported: "The vacuum brake was fitted a few years ago to the J. R. & T. stock, but the coal consumption went up so rapidly, due to the working of the ejector, that its use was soon discontinued; the fittings are, however, still retained, but at the present time the engines are equipped with powerful steam brakes". Thoroughly progressive in nearly every other respect, it is surprising that the company should have taken such a retrograde step as to abandon the use of a continuous brake. No mention of the fact has been found in the company's minutes. The writer can confirm from photographs in his possession that the brake pipes had been removed from the engines by 1930 and it is believed that this was done some years earlier.

On 9 February 1905 the manager drew attention to the recent developments of motor omnibuses and rail motors; representatives of the railway and the Jersey Eastern made a tour in England and France to study the matter. The suggestion was made that the companies should protect themselves by forming an auxiliary motor omnibus company, but no resolution was passed and nothing further was heard of the idea.

In the autumn of 1906 Mr. Ramsey Kendal, manager of the North Eastern Railway Company's locomotive works at Darlington, was asked to examine the J. R. & T. locomotives and rolling stock. He gave details and the cause of every delay to traffic which had occurred since December 1905, and stated that although there had been a series of temporary stoppages he did not think they had been caused by any neglect on the part of those concerned with the upkeep of the engines, as they appeared to be intelligently and skilfully looked after. The mishaps were no more serious than those occurring on other railways, but unfortunately they were more noticeable on a small line with limited rolling stock, especially as in this case they all happened within a comparatively short period. He had examined the four engines very carefully and also the carriages and brake vans, and although the engines were very light for the work they had to do, they were in good working order. Some of the carriage bogies were of an antiquated pattern but these, he understood, were being gradually replaced as funds permitted.

It was resolved that a new and more powerful engine be purchased. Mr. Dickson produced six tenders for the proposed new locomotive, and on his recommendation it was decided to accept that of Messrs. Andrew Barclay, of Kilmarnock, for an 8-wheeled locomotive, delivered to Jersey for the sum of £1,750. Later he came to the conclusion that owing to the extra long wheelbase, an 8-wheeled locomotive was going to necessitate a great many alterations to the permanent way and was also going to cancel out the benefit of the proposed workshop alterations. It was, therefore, decided to order the 6-wheeled one tendered for by the same firm at a cost of £1,710.

At the 1907 annual general meeting of the company the chairman explained that electrification of the line had been very seriously considered during the previous year, and that an electrical corporation in London had been negotiating to find the necessary capital and execute the work under certain conditions, but the directors had decided that steam traction would be best and most economical for the purpose at present, and in consequence a new locomotive had been ordered to cope with the heavy summer traffic.

The New Station at Millbrook

In September 1910 a proposed siding immediately beyond First Tower Station, the new position of the line from First Tower to Millbrook, and a siding at Millbrook were all approved. The new station at Millbrook was opened on 15 January 1912. The extension of Victoria Avenue from Millbrook to Bel Royal and the consequent alterations to the railway did not take place until some time after the conclusion of World War I.

Mr. Dickson informed the board on 7 October 1912 that as several new roof lamps were required he had gone into the question of lighting a train by electricity. A month later he was authorised to proceed with the installation of Stone's lighting system in five carriages.

At about the same time the Mitchelite Air Gas Company offered to supply a lighting plant for Millbrook station at virtually cost price on condition that prospective customers should be allowed to inspect it. The price of £20 included a guarantee for 12 months and it was decided to accept the offer.

On 22 March 1913 a severe gale sprang up during the afternoon, when there was an unusually high spring tide. The 6-5 p.m. train from St. Helier was unable to proceed beyond Bel Royal, whence it backed to Millbrook for shelter and eventually returned to St. Helier at 8-40 p.m. It left again at 9-5 p.m. and reached St. Aubin at 10-15 p.m., the platelayers clearing the line ahead of it as it crawled along. The

6-12 p.m. train from Corbiere was held up at St. Aubin, the ballast having been washed out of the track in places to a depth of two feet. This train managed to continue its journey at 10-20 p.m., and was followed by the usual 10-30 p.m., which made its final journey from St. Helier at 11 p.m. for Don Bridge. Between 6-15 and 8-30 p.m. heavy seas broke continuously over the Esplanade, and at one time there was a foot of water on the track in St. Helier terminus.

Following the lengthening some months previously of the platform at St. Helier by 50 feet, it was decided to spend approximately £300 on a new carriage shed at St. Aubin, together with a porter's room, water tower and crane and a platelayer's store. Mr. Dickson reported that the installation of electric light in some of the carriages had proved satisfactory and it was, therefore, decided to equip the remainder at an estimated cost of £300. A third brake van had been fitted with dynamo and accumulators, and all the carriages were fully equipped by the end of the year.

At the 18th annual general meeting on 6 February 1914, the chairman was able to report a total of 726,390 passengers carried during the year 1913, exclusive of season ticket holders. There had been record takings and a record profit, which enabled a dividend of 4 per cent to be paid on the ordinary shares. He stated that steps were being taken to augment the facilities for dealing with the traffic, and that two additional carriages were being built. He also mentioned that carriages could be built locally at 50 per cent less than English prices, a recent mainland tender for one carriage being higher than the price paid in 1897 for two.

Colonel Snowdon Robin, who had joined the board in 1899 and had been chairman for many years, died in December 1914. He was succeeded by Mr. E. C. Moore, an Alderman of the City of London, and director for many years, who stated at the annual general meeting on 12 February 1915 that everyone must realise that the company had suffered very seriously owing to the war, as the "haymaking season" was just beginning when war broke out in the previous August, and the preparations that had been made to deal with a record traffic were largely wasted. The few visitors in Jersey at the beginning of August were "practically ordered out of the Island". The takings were £1,863 down, but economies in working amounted to £942.

German Prisoners-of-War

Considerable interest was aroused locally when it became known that a contingent of German prisoners-of-war was due to arrive at St. Helier during the early morning of 20 March 1915, and shortly after 6 a.m. H.M.S. *Lydia* (formerly the London & South Western Railway cross-channel steamer) entered the harbour. In due course the prisoners, totalling 596 men, began to file across the gangway and lined up in fours on the quayside. A total of over 30 sick and wounded were the last to land and were driven to their destination. The remainder were formed into three columns, which marched off at intervals of about 10 minutes. The first was "entrained in the carriages that were standing in the siding facing Messrs. Moore's store, while the two next to march up went along the railway line to the platform, alongside which two other trains were standing, and all three trains were got off within the space of 35 to 40 minutes". The destination was Blanches Banques, where wooden huts had been erected. A further batch of about 500 men arrived two days later, when special trains, all from the station platform, were scheduled to leave at 9 a.m., 9-15 and 9-35 a.m.

Work was arranged for many of the prisoners at the docks in St. Helier, and they were conveyed backwards and forwards by special train. In the early morning this ran empty and non-stop from St. Helier to Don Bridge, where the engine was uncoupled, ran round the train, was re-coupled and then backed the train to Blanches Banques, in readiness to receive the prisoners. At Don Bridge the St. Helier—Corbiere train was passed, and the "special" then ran non-stop to St. Helier in 18 minutes. The same train took the men back to camp for lunch, then returned to Don Bridge, waited there in the loop after the engine had run round the train, in due course backed to Blanches Banques, re-embarked the prisoners, and on this occasion was scheduled to take 23 minutes for the journey to St. Helier, passing the 2 p.m. train from St. Helier at Millbrook. It was considered inadvisable to stop the train en route in case any of the prisoners should

Overbridge at Seven Oaks, between St. Aubin and Pont Marquet, built
in 1875 by the St. Aubin's & La Moye Railway

Constructing   the
tunnel at St. Aubin

No. 2, St. 'Aubyns', at Don Bridge. Note the crossing loop

A. Brunden–Langley

No. 2 and train at St. Aubin before the opening of the tunnel in 1898

Corbiere lighthouse, showing the railway terminus in right-hand middle background

Advocate Lempriere

No. 5, 'La Moye', at Corbiere about 1908

A. J. LeMottée

The accident at La Moye Quarries in 1895. Locomotive No. 1 'St. Heliers'

'*The Pioneer No. 2*', *being towed from the Albert Quay, St. Helier, on arrival in 1924*

'*The Pioneer No. 2*', *painted yellow, at Corbiere during the trial run. The tall man on the left of the platform is Mr. W. N. Poingdestre, the manager*

'*The Pioneer No. 1*' *and* '*The Pioneer No. 2*' *at Millbrook*

A. Labbé

The locomotive 'North Western' sold to the Jersey Eastern Railway in 1878

1st class bogie car
(No. 12) 1887

Composite bogie car
with central gangway
(No. 9) 1884

4-wheel brake van
(No. 11) 1884

(Photo by makers:
Bristol Wagon &
Carriage Works)

'No. 1 at St. Helier after rebuilding

Miss Vilton

No. 5, 'La Moye'. *The grease on the side tanks suggests that the photograph was taken very soon after arrival in Jersey*

No. 1 arriving at St. Helier in 1930. Note acetylene headlamp and absence of vacuum brake pipe

The original 'General Don' when running on the W.C. & P.R. Note outside cylinders

Bogie first and second class composite carriage, showing title shortened to "Jersey Railway" and monogram introduced about 1930

Railcar 'Normandy' approaching the Corbiere platform at St. Aubin. Note green and cream colour scheme introduced about 1931

No. 4 'St. Brelades', near Blanches Banques in 1913, showing extra coach, 4-wheel brake and standard train set. Note acetylene container in front of side tank

escape, the method adopted by the driver being to proceed slowly as far as St. Aubin, keeping a close watch for the 2 o'clock train and when that was seen to be approaching First Tower to give the engine full throttle and run through Millbrook at about 25 miles an hour just after the other train had pulled into the loop. Some smart running usually took place in the evening as, after returning the prisoners to Blanches Banques, the train was backed to Don Bridge, the engine ran round, was recoupled and the empty train left at about 6-10 p.m., it being necessary to reach St. Helier before the departure of the 6-30 p.m. ordinary train for St. Aubin.

The prisoners left the island in February 1917 but it is believed that further batches arrived in due course. The company was able to pay a 3 per cent ordinary dividend in 1915, and in all probability this not-unfavourable state of affairs was due in large measure to the revenue obtained from these special trains. Traffic decreased considerably in 1916 and 1917 so that no ordinary dividend was paid in either year and none on the cumulative preference shares in 1917. There was no ordinary dividend in 1918, but the 4 per cent preference dividend was brought up to date.

A joint meeting of the boards of the J. R. & T. and J.E.R. was held on 21 May 1919 to petition the States to allow an increase in fares to 1½*d.* a mile second class and 2½*d.* a mile first class, plus an additional ½*d.* a mile in each class between St. Aubin and Corbiere. The Bill was passed by the States on 26 June, the new charges to be in operation for a period of six years.

The New Station at Bel.Royal

In August 1919 the Main Roads Committee brought up the matter of the continuation of Victoria Avenue from Millbrook to Bel Royal, asking the railway company to move the station and line at Bel Royal; these extensions and alterations had been held up owing to the war. The board expressed the opinion that the new site could only be a temporary one as, when a further extension of the sea wall to Beaumont was contemplated, a second move to a permanent site would no doubt become necessary. It referred to a stipulation made

in 1912 that the existing station at Bel Royal should be moved at
public cost, that a new platform 100 feet longer than the existing
one should be provided, that the new track formation be properly
ballasted to receive sleepers, and that the new land should be
conveyed to the company in exchange for the deeds of the old land,
the company only paying the cost of the new sleepers and rails.
These conditions were agreed to and in due course the change-over
was made.

During the war, money that would normally have been spent
on upkeep was used to increase wages and buy coal to keep the
engines going. Coal had been a very expensive item in 1919, the cost
being $2\frac{1}{2}$ times as much as it was in 1913. The number of passengers
carried during the year was 15,000 fewer than in 1913, but the passenger
train mileage was only 58,801 as against 80,175. Revenue exceeded
that of the previous year by £4,781 and of 1913 by £2,702. A dividend
of 4 per cent was paid on the ordinary shares, the chairman announ-
cing that it would be necessary to spend £7,000 during the next few
years to get the line into proper working order.

Towards the end of 1920 the board wrote to the Great Western
Railway asking for an expert to report on the company's organisation
and efficiency. The gentleman in question, Mr. R. R. P. Glover of
Slough, presented a report on 24 January 1921. The exact details are
not available, but arising out of it, it was decided at the next board
meeting, not to proceed with negotiations for the sale of locomotive
No. 5 *La Moye* in view of the fact that it was likely to be of great
service as soon as the permanent way had been strengthened. It was
also stated that the painting, varnishing and upholstering of the
carriages were in progress as were the repairing and painting of the
wagons; additional men were to be engaged for the purpose of completing the repairs to the roof of St. Helier station; instructions were
given to proceed with the erection of a shelter at La Moye station.
The latter and La Haule became ticket-issuing stations on 30 September
1921. It was also decided at this time that the platform at West Park
be lengthened to take a full train, thus saving the necessity of pulling
up twice, as hitherto.

In 1921 Mr. W. H. Dickson retired, and his deputy, Mr. W. N.

Poingdestre was appointed secretary and manager as from 1
September.

Horse Racing took place near Don Bridge on August Bank
Holiday 1921, a total of 12,307 passengers being carried on that day,
the takings amounting to £368. During the week 38,920 passengers
were carried and the takings were £1,030. A new shelter was erected
on the Corbiere line platform at St. Aubin to serve as a waiting room
and enable the old roof to be demolished, on the grounds that is was
unsafe.

On 24 February 1922 the board considered drawings and estimates
for Tilling-Stevens electric rail cars and Brill petrol rail cars, the
manager being asked to obtain fuller details of these and of the Sentinel-
Cammell steam system. Three months later Sentinel suggested that a
special coach or truck should be built for experimental use on the
J. R. & T., provided the latter agreed to pay the freight both ways
should they wish to return the vehicle for alterations or because it
had proved unsuitable. The company accepted this offer and at the
end of November 1922, a representative each of the Sentinel Waggon
Works Limited and of Cammell, Laird & Company Limited arrived
in Jersey to obtain details of local conditions. Shortly afterwards a
quotation of £1,800 was submitted for a large type of rail car, as
compared with £1,500 for a smaller one discussed previously, and
this was accepted subject to delivery in Jersey by 1 April 1923.

Introduction of Bus Services

An event of great importance to the Island, and to the J. R. & T.
in particular, took place on Easter Monday, 2 April 1923, when the
Jersey Motor Transport Company Limited started operations with a
fleet of motor omnibuses which served all parts of the Island. Routes
competing directly with the J. R. & T. were those from St. Helier
to St. Aubin, St. Brelade's Bay and Corbiere, and it may be added
that the Jersey Eastern Railway suffered severely from other services.
The J. R. & T. board decided at a meeting held a week before the
bus service started that they would have to reduce their fares and the
following advertisement was inserted in the local newspapers:—"In

view of increased facilities for handling traffic economically, the company gives notice that a reduced scale of fares will be notified at an early date". The increased facilities mentioned were in connection with the forthcoming introduction of the rail cars.

On 1 August 1923 the J. R. & T. inaugurated their own service of buses between St. Aubin and St. Brelade's Bay, to connect with the trains and act as feeders. To begin with two French-built buses were employed, but before long others were purchased in France and England and additional routes were placed in operation.

The intention expressed in 1896 to open a station at Bellozanne, remained in abeyance until 1923, when it was decided to give the name "Bellozanne Halt" to the platform that was being built near "Tyneville". It was also decided to lease a strip of land from the owner of "Beau Rivage", Beaumont, in order to erect "Bel Royal Halt" for the use of the rail cars. At about the same time, "Millbrook Halt" between First Tower and Millbrook, and "Beaumont Halt" between Beaumont and La Haule were completed for a similar purpose.

The Sentinel Rail Cars

The experimental Sentinel-Cammell steam railcar, named *The Pioneer No. 1* was late in arriving, but was assembled in time to make its inaugural run on 18 June 1923, when a representative group of islanders travelled in it from St. Helier to St. Aubin and back. "Whether running at 35 miles an hour, as it did for part of the journey, or slowing down at the curves, there was the same absence of friction." Apart from the one short burst of speed, the car was allowed to proceed in a leisurely manner and St. Aubin was reached in 12 minutes. Several further trips were made during the afternoon and evening, and "after some necessary work has been attended to it will be put in regular use". It looks as if the reporter who wrote this last sentence was unaware that the leading axle snapped during the final trial run. At an enquiry the manager of Cammell Laird expressed the opinion that the mishap had been caused by a defect in workmanship or material, as this type of axle was designed to withstand a strain of 180 tons.

The railcar was 56 ft. 6 in. long and weighed 15 tons 13 cwt. in working order. The two cylinders, 6¾ ins. diameter by 9 ins. stroke, were connected to the power bogie by single-chain gearing, the boiler pressure being 230 lb. per square inch. When travelling forwards it was controlled by a driver-cum-fireman, but in the opposite direction required in addition the services of the guard who acted as a brakesman. Accommodation was provided for 64 passengers, the reversible seats in the first class compartment being upholstered in royal blue plush and those in the second class in bronze-coloured cloth.

The necessary repairs were effected in time for a party of British and foreign engineers to make a trial run from St. Helier to St. Aubin and back on 28 June 1923. The party included four representatives each from Czecho-Slovakia and Denmark, two from Norway and one each from Austria and Mexico, all these guests and a number of others being entertained to lunch at the Grand Hotel. Mr. G. Butler Lloyd of Sentinel presided and congratulated the J. R. & T. on being the first concern to make use of the new rail car, which he believed had a great future.

There is no doubt that much credit is due to the J. R. & T. for placing the railcar in service, but between the years 1903 and 1911 no fewer than 20 railways in the British Isles had introduced direct-drive steam railcars, a number of which were still in service when Sentinel-Cammell introduced their particular design using experience gained by Sentinel in some twenty years' manufacture of steam road lorries. Within a few years the steam railcar was doomed to be superseded by the diesel-electric unit.

The summer service introduced in the middle of the month provided no fewer than 32 weekday trains between St. Helier and St. Aubin, and of these nine proceeded to Corbiere and back. With few exceptions there were two trains an hour to and from St. Aubin. On the occasion of the races at Don Bridge on 26 July an even more intensive timetable was put into operation, and there were 23 trains from St. Helier to Don Bridge and vice versa at a fare of 1/3d. return. At one stage in the day there were eight departures from St. Helier in the space of two hours, namely, at 11-0, 11-5, 11-15, and 11-30 a.m., 12-5, 12-27, 12-35 and 1-0 p.m., and of these one train proceeded as far as St. Aubin only, five to Don Bridge and two to Don Bridge and Corbiere.

The Pioneer, No. 2 a new car embodying improvements suggested by the first trials, arrived in Jersey early in January 1924 and on the 17th was tested on the steep gradients between St. Aubin and Corbiere. It was considerably more powerful than its predecessor and was fitted with double-chain gearing, which was a very desirable safeguard when negotiating gradients of 1 in 40 or steeper; in view of its single chain gearing "No. 1" car had only been despatched to Corbiere very occasionally. At a further trial of the new car on 20 February, representatives from Australia and France and from the London, Midland & Scottish Railway were present. In an after-dinner speech Mr. Poingdestre mentioned that the railcars could each make four single journeys between St. Helier and St. Aubin in an hour, this being impossible with the ordinary locomotives because of the time taken in running round the train after each journey. From June 1923 to date, "No. 1" car had run 12,700 miles on 70 tons of coal, and it was satisfactory to note that a locomotive would have consumed 350 tons on the same mileage. The railcar was consuming 5 lb. of coal a mile as against 25 lb. for a locomotive.

"No. 3" railcar, which was often referred to as the "Wembley" car because it had been on view at Wembley Exhibition, arrived in Jersey in March 1925, and made a trial run to Corbiere on 8 April with satisfactory results. Its official name was *La Moye*, as the locomotive of that name was no longer in service; it is believed that by this time railcar "No. 2" had been renamed *Portēlet*.

A Successful Year

The year 1925 was undoubtedly the most successful in the company's history. Passenger traffic receipts were £22,265 and total revenue £23,475, an increase of £2,349 over the previous year. Working expenses and provision for maintenance were £21,000. A dividend of 7 per cent was declared on the ordinary shares. The train mileage was 112,147 as compared with 80,175 in 1913; the daily number of trains in each direction 33 as compared with 19, the quantity of coal consumed 1,216 tons as against 1,325 (the reduction being due, of course, to the advent of the railcars) and the number of passengers carried 1,091,789 as against 726,390.

The adverse effect that private cars were having on the company was stressed for the first time at the 1928 annual general meeting, when Sir William Vernon, who had been re-elected to the board following his resignation, after many years, from the post of Bailiff, mentioned that during the past 18 months the numbers of cars on the roads had increased almost beyond conception. Farmers and labourers now had their own small car, whereas they formerly walked to the station and proceeded by train into town.

It was announced that negotiations between the J. R. & T. and the Jersey Motor Transport Company Limited had been successfully concluded and that the former would take over the latter as from 5 August 1928, from which date tickets for buses and trains would be interchangeable. The purchase was financed by means of £16,000 worth of 5 per cent notes; the assets of the J.M.T. included 17 motor vehicles.

At the 1929 annual general meeting the chairman, after talking about the acquisition of the J.M.T. referred to the severity of the competition with which they were being faced by the extension of road services in the West. "I can assure you", he said "now that the trouble has ceased, that the competition gave your directors grave cause for anxiety. We were faced either with a cut-throat rate war or some scheme of co-operation with our principal competitor."

The chairman went on to say that many members of the travelling public preferred the road vehicle to the train, and that this was true to such an extent that they had found it useless during the winter months to run trains to Corbiere while maintaining a parallel service by road. But they were bound by statute to run a minimum number of trains daily to this destination, and at a later stage of the meeting a petition to the States was read asking that the company be allowed to suspend their rail service between St. Aubin and Corbiere from the end of September to the beginning of May and to modify their fares.

The Jersey Eastern Railway closed down for good on 21 June,

1929. Although latterly they had been operating two Sentinel railcars, they had delayed too long before introducing them and had been equally slow in starting their own bus service. Almost a year previously, on 7 August 1928, the J. R. & T. board had considered a letter from the J.E.R. proposing an amalgamation of the two concerns, but after the matter had been gone into very thoroughly the suggestion was wisely turned down. When the J.E.R. equipment and rolling stock came into the market, the J. R. & T. made an offer of £100 for the railcar *Normandy* and eventually, in July 1930, succeeded in purchasing it for this very reasonable sum.

Winter Closure

On 5 January 1931 a petition was sent to the States for the suspension of the service between St. Helier and St. Aubin each winter from 1 October to 30 April, and at the annual general meeting on 27 February, it was stated that gross receipts were lower by £2,400, and a net loss of £825 had been incurred, mainly due to the competition of road transport. Private cars were carrying the type of passenger who used to fill the first class carriages; the ever-increasing number of char-a-bancs competed for the summer traffic, and worst of all the buses had taken away much of the second class traffic.

As a result of a tragic accident on 27 June 1931 to a small J.M.T. bus, which got out of control when descending Mont Felard Hill and overturned at the bottom, Mr. Poingdestre offered his resignation as secretary and manager of the J. R. & T. and J.M.T. and the board felt obliged to accept it. These two posts were taken over by Mr. F. H. Blakeway.

Sanction to the Bill dealing with the winter closure of the Corbiere extension arrived in time for the rail service from St. Aubin to Corbiere to be discontinued as from 1 October 1931. Trains began to run again on 1 May 1932 and similar arrangements applied in subsequent years.

No ordinary dividend was paid for the year 1931. The principal reasons given by the chairman were the very wet summer and the poor state of repair of the buses, which had been the company's principal money-earners. He went on to say that Mr. Poingdestre was a railwayman and had not received any training in motor transport. As the bus services had become all-important it was clearly necessary to appoint as manager someone with experience of motor transport. Since 1 January 1932 the 13 J. R. & T. omnibuses had been leased to the J.M.T. for three years at an annual rental of £2,000. A Bill to suspend the winter rail service between St. Helier and St. Aubin was still before the States.

The Main Roads Committee finally agreed that the rail service might be suspended from 1 December 1932 to 30 April 1933 but stipulations were made that there should be at least a dozen bus departures in each direction between St. Helier and St. Aubin, weekdays and Sundays alike, and that there should be no increase in fares.

Big Drop in Revenue

At the 1933 annual general meeting the chairman referred to the considerable changes in the balance sheet, due largely to the fact that the old service of blue buses had been taken over by the J.M.T. Even after crediting the hire charge of £2,000 there was a reduction in revenue of no less than £8,170 in 1932 as compared with 1931, the greater part of this being due to the transfer of the bus service. Operating expenses had been reduced by £6,357, and other economies made the total saving £7,472. The net results of working the railway were worse than the previous year by nearly £700. However, an overall loss of £875 on the year's working had been turned into a profit of £842 by crediting profit on the sale of an investment in a subsidiary company and part of this sum was used in payment of a dividend of 1½ per cent on the ordinary shares.

Application was again made in July 1933 to run buses instead of trains between St. Helier and St. Aubin during the following winter, and the service was suspended between 1 October and 30 April. Similar arrangements were made in 1934 and again in 1935, but in the former year the board decided to run a special half-hourly service by railcar between St. Helier and St. Aubin on 21, 22, and 24 December; the experiment was not repeated. As, however, the main road between Beaumont and La Haule was closed to all traffic for repairs in January 1936, a service by railcar was operated during the period of closure between St. Aubin and Beaumont, where connection was made with the buses to and from St. Helier.

The results of the year 1933 were somewhat better than those of 1932, but no ordinary dividend was possible. There was a loss of £1,325 in 1934, due largely to the fact that no dividend was received from the J.M.T. The chairman was extremely outspoken in his remarks: "For years past we have been subjected to the fiercest competition that any commercial enterprise has ever faced. It was quite obvious that our principal competitor was out to drive us off the road, hampered as we have been by the railway round our necks. To have given in to such competition would have been to abandon once and for all any hope of the shareholders ever getting one penny of their capital back. The folly of such extreme competition had by now become obvious to both sides and in the autumn we succeeded in making a treaty of peace and friendship with our chief opponents, under which we took the west and they the east of the Island, as sole territory. We were naturally loath to lose districts where the J.M.T. had been the pioneer of bus traffic, but there is no doubt whatever that this division was in our best interests. You must not think that we have a monopoly, or even such an advantage that we can yet raise fares from their present absurdly low level. On the contrary three bus enterprises are still outside the agreement and are in active competition therewith". The principal competitor referred to by the chairman was the Safety Coach Service Limited, which had started operations in 1927.

The beneficial results of the agreement were first shown in the 1935 accounts, which indicated a profit of £952 as compared with a loss of £1,325 in 1934, so this was equivalent to an improvement of £2,277. It must, however, be pointed out that the Company had received a cash payment of £1,750 from the J.M.T., due to the fact that they carried free a large number of passengers holding interchangeable return bus tickets, without receiving any corresponding advantage. A far-reaching result of the agreement was that laws were

introduced to regulate the entire Island bus industry. A dividend of
2½ per cent was paid on the J. R. & T. ordinary shares.

In March 1936 a request was sent to the Great Western for an
engineer to inspect the permanent way. His report started with the
reassuring statement: "Bearing in mind the circumstances under
which your traffic is worked, and the plant which operates on it, I
am of opinion that your railway is adequately maintained and will be
in a condition to satisfactorily carry the public when the local repairs
following the present high tides and certain works which are recorded
herein are complete". Two of the criticisms made by the States'
engineer were that there were many lengths of straight rail on curved
sections and that these had resisted bending, and that some rails on
curves were too short. The inspecting engineer agreed with these
views, and expressed the opinion that the badly-pitted 70 lb. rails
near Beaumont should be renewed. He ended: "The speed of your
trains is low and the weights of your vehicles light, and the greater
part of the necessary immediate work to be done is alignment. I
understand that you are opening for traffic on 1 May next and I
recommend that your maintenance gang be strengthened by four men
until that date to cope with the work".

The train service from St. Helier—St. Aubin—Corbiere was
duly resumed on 1 May 1936 and closed down for the winter
on 30 September 1936. As customary, almost the entire rolling
stock, apart from the railcars and locomotives, was stored at St.
Aubin.

Fire Brings the End

A disastrous fire broke out in St. Aubin's station during the early
hours of Sunday morning, 18 October 1936, believed to have been
caused by some faulty electrical equipment in a butcher's shop, which
had been built a short time previously along the wall of the station
facing the main road. The fire was fanned by a strong breeze, spread
with alarming rapidity and seriously endangered the lives of the
handful of people living at the Terminus Hotel. They were roused
just in time but part of the hotel was badly damaged. Five shops were

completely destroyed as were the station roof and no fewer than 16 carriages, including most of the latest and best.

The board wasted no time in deciding that it would be undesirable if not impossible to continue railway operations, and on 2 November 1936 wrote as follows to the Main Roads Committee:—

"The fire which occurred in the early morning of the 18th October, and destroyed not only the station and carriage sheds at St. Aubin, but the larger part of the passenger carriages belonging to this company, has led the board to make a careful study of the future of the railway enterprise, which has served the public for the past 66 years under the control of your Committee.

"The board has come to the conclusion that an arrangement by which the States would take over the concessions and real estates of the company on terms to be arranged, offers very great advantages, financial and other, to the public of the Island, while at the same time offering to the shareholders an opportunity —even at a loss of part of their capital— of paying off the debts due by the company."

The Committee wrote on 2 January 1937 to say that they would be prepared to recommend the States to offer a sum of £25,000 for the transfer of the whole of the company's interests in the concessions and real estates. At an extraordinary general meeting on February 15, the chairman emphasised the necessity for accepting the offer. "After trying every expedient this railway cannot be made to pay. Nor does the future offer any prospect of better conditions; on the contrary they are getting worse. Our good old locomotives are getting on in years, and there is no means whatever for providing for their replacement, nor for that of the railcars. To replace the burnt rolling stock we have only the small sum received from the insurance.

"Such was the position of affairs after the fire ocurred at St. Aubin last October. The result of this is, after reinstating the hotel, to provide a sum of about £7,500 in cash. This, of course, belongs to the creditors and cannot be used otherwise than for reinstatement or for paying off debt. But the existence of this sum in cash does facilitate the sale of the rest of the purely railway property.

"So the board took steps to obtain a cash offer for the railway property and concessions. I may add that the rails, rolling stock and other moveables are not included in these negotiations as we hope to realise these to better advantage ourselves if the concessions are sold. Partly owing to the unfortunate fact that the gauge of the line is not standard, it is not hoped to get a large sum for these. We hope for roughly £3,000.

"Now, if our titles were in order the disposal of the line would cause the board no anxiety whatever. But the founders of the company, 66 years ago, did not get good titles, thinking no doubt that the railway would go on for ever. So that, as far as West Park we are leaseholders only, whilst from there to St. Aubin inclusive our title is open to doubt. The La Moye section has a good title but is of comparatively small value. All this boils down to the unpleasant fact that the only buyer who can safely take the risk of buying is the States, and that body is well aware of it.

"With the sale of rails, etc., and the realisation of assets other than the J.M.T. we hope to get together about enough cash to pay off the debentures, notes and other creditors. This will leave the J.M.T., the only really live part of our business, for the preference and ordinary shareholders.

"For legal reasons we have to liquidate the old J. R. & T. Company after the sale, but to do this without putting the J.M.T. also into liquidation would require the formation of a fresh holding company, to which the J.M.T. would be transferred, and the holding company's shares given in exchange to the present railway shareholders. As to results, these would appear likely to be much better than at present as the large, and as I have shown increasing, losses on the railway swallow up most of the bus profits. Relieved from the railway losses we shall only have against us the rent, £1,050 per annum, of this station and the garage at St. Aubin, which are absolutely essential for the working of the bus service. Part of the bargain is that we shall have for the J.M.T. a 25 year lease on these premises."

A resolution was then carried unanimously. At the 41st annual general meeting held on 1 March 1937 an ordinary dividend of 2½ per cent was declared in addition to the 4 per cent preference dividend, for the year 1936.

Tenders were considered on 5 July, for the rails, sleepers, fishplates, four locomotives, three railcars, carriages and brake vans, that of

Messrs. George Cohen being accepted for £5,915. This firm took immediate steps to carry out their side of the bargain. Only three railcars were included, as No. 1 had been placed on the disposal list in 1935, and meanwhile must either have been sold or scrapped.

An extraordinary general meeting was held on 28 October 1937 to pass resolutions that the company be wound up and the directors authorised to sell all the realty to the States of Jersey for £25,000; that outstanding debentures and notes should be redeemed at par; to transfer to the newly-formed company, Jersey Road Transport Limited (of which the then directors of the J. R. & T. Ltd. were the first directors) all the shares of the J.M.T. Company registered in the name of the J. R. & T. This marked the finish of a small but quite remarkable company. It remains to give some fuller details of loco-motives, rolling stock, permanent way, etc.

Locomotives (4 ft. 8½ in. gauge)

Although it seems abundantly clear that not more than twelve locomotives and four steam railcars were owned by the Jersey Railway Company and its successors between the years 1870 and 1936, the majority of stock lists published hitherto have contained errors or omissions. Doubts still exist about certain standard and narrow gauge locomotives.

As regards the former, it is quite certain that the first two—No. 1, *Haro Haro* (Works No. 2047) and No. 2 *Duke of Normandy* (Works No. 2048)—were delivered by Sharp Stewart in September 1870. They were 2-4-0 tank engines, with leading wheels 2 ft. and coupled wheels 4 ft. in diameter, the total wheelbase being 11 ft. Cylinders were 10 in. x 16 in.

The *British Press & Jersey Times* of 9 June 1871 announced the arrival of a new engine and said that the total was three. The same newspaper of 14 September 1875, in reporting a slight mishap to *Haro Haro* stated that the other two engines were both under repair. In other words, according to the man on the spot the total was still three and one would certainly expect him to be correct.

The North British Locomotive Company Limited, the successors to Sharp Stewart, have kindly gone to considerable trouble to sort things out. The first thing to mention is that Works No. 2149, sometimes stated to have been built for the Jersey Railway, was in fact delivered to the Furness Railway and bore no resemblance to the engines used in Jersey.

Sharp Stewart took an order in 1870 for a 2-4-0 tank having 12 in. x 17 in. cylinders and driving wheels of 4 ft. diameter; the Works No. was 2140. In 1871 an exactly similar order—also for Jersey—was taken for an engine to which Works No. 2241 was allotted. These two engines had a total wheelbase of 12 ft. 5 in., larger boilers than the original pair and, unlike them, each had a dome.

The writer has in his possession an excellent photograph (reproduced on another page) of a 2-4-0 tank named *North Western* and has had the bottom left hand corner, containing the number plate, considerably enlarged. The wording is very clear and it is

practically certain that the Works No. shown is 2241. Unfortunately the
North British Company have no record when this engine was delivered,
but it is a reasonable assumption that No. 2140 was completed before
No. 2241 and was the engine referred to in the newspaper report.

What then of No. 2241, *North Western*, and why that name?
A partial answer is that it was named after the North Western Railway
Company (of Jersey), which, as stated earlier, was promoted at a
meeting held in January 1872 and was intended to run (but never did)
from Don Bridge (or Don Farm as the locality was then called) to St.
Peter and beyond. Nearly a year earlier the first steps had been taken
to establish the St. Aubin's & La Moye Railway Company, whose
route between the places in its title was to be via Don Farm, which
meant that the North Western Railway would connect at the last
named point. It is evident that the line was to be built to standard
gauge, and what more likely than an order being placed almost at
once for an engine to assist in the construction? This had not been
necessary in the case of the Jersey Railway as the line was almost dead
level, whereas the new line had extremely steep gradients and various
earthworks were unavoidable. In view of the initial desire on the part of
the St. Aubin's & La Moye to co-operate with the North Western it
was very appropriate for the former to name their engine *North Western*.

It could not have been foreseen that work on the St. Aubin's &
La Moye Railway would not start until August 1873, and that it
would proceed very slowly. The first mention of any rails being laid
occurred in 1876, but it is not known whether these were standard or
narrow gauge. It is, however, certain that by July 1877 the railway
was being built to 3 ft. 6 in. gauge and one is justified in assuming
that *North Western* had been transferred to the Jersey Railway track.
Whether it was employed thereon or merely stored is not known.
As the company apparently had three other engines and the line
was only 3¾ miles long with one passing loop at Millbrook, and the
normal frequency of service being hourly, one would have thought
that it would have been difficult to find regular employment for the
newcomer. In any event, the engine was removed on 21 June 1878
from the Jersey Railway to the Jersey Eastern Railway, by whom it
had been purchased.

The North British Company has confirmed that a 2-4-0 tank was built by Dubs in 1878-79 and was named *General Don*; this engine had 10 in. x 18 in. cylinders and 4 ft. driving wheels. A likely reason—it is difficult to find a better—why the *North Western* was disposed of and *General Don* ordered is that the Jersey Eastern Railway was in urgent need of additional motive power at this time and the sale was agreed to as a friendly gesture. It was, however, considered necessary to order another engine to take its place—which suggests that the *North Western* did run for the Jersey Railway.

A photograph of a farewell party to the manager, Mr. R. B. Carnegy, in July 1883 clearly shows the *Duke of Normandy* together with an engine of similar appearance but in an unpainted condition, and therefore without a name—undoubtedly the *Haro Haro* as these were the only two which looked alike. The pair—probably assisted by *General Don* and possibly by No. 3—is believed to have run between St. Helier and St. Aubin (latterly from St. Helier to First Tower only) until September 1884, when the change from standard to narrow gauge was completed. All were withdrawn and the *Duke of Normandy* and *Haro Haro* eventually served as contractor's locomotives in the building of the Manchester Ship Canal. Later the former was sold to Mr. T. W. Ward of Sheffield, who in turn sold it in 1897 to the Vulcan Foundry Company, by whom it was employed until 1904, when it was scrapped. The *General Don* became the *Clevedon* of the Weston, Clevedon & Portishead Railway and survived until 1940. It will be seen from one of the accompanying photographs that, unlike the other standard gauge engines, it was fitted with outside cylinders.

The Locomotive stated that some six-coupled saddle tanks were purchased to replace the engines just mentioned and that they worked the line until the gauge was narrowed in 1884, when they were disposed of. Bearing in mind the photograph taken in 1883, it seems unlikely that any such engines existed.

Locomotives (3 ft. 6 ins. gauge)

By July 1877 or earlier the St. Aubin's & La Moye line was being built to 3 ft. 6 ins. gauge. Two months later it was announced that *General Don*, the first of two engines being built for the line, was being assembled at St. Aubin and the first trial trip took place on 10 September. Work on the railway was suspended from December 1877 for more than five years, and during this time the engines came into the possession of the Viscount following bankruptcy.

When work was resumed in 1883, the line was completed from a temporary terminus near St. Aubin's Hospital to La Moye in time for a trial trip on 15 March 1884, when it can be assumed that the *General Don* or the companion engine provided the motive power.

Unfortunately, no contemporary descriptions of these engines have been discovered, but the following paragraph appeared in *The Locomotive* for 15 January 1914:—"The first engines for the 3 ft. 6 ins. gauge were some 0-4-2 saddle tanks built by Black, Hawthorn & Company, and had outside cylinders 11 ins. x 18 ins. Apparently they were originally used by the contractors who narrowed the gauge and built the Corbiere Extension Line. They stood idle at St. Helier for many years, being finally sold in 1899 or 1900". All this fits in perfectly; and the writer is fortunate in being able to reproduce a photograph of what is undoubtedly one of them.

What does seem rather strange is that one engine should have been named *General Don* and that the Jersey Railway should have chosen the same name for their standard-gauge engine of 1878-79. Such a duplication could of course have happened, particularly as General Don was very much in the thoughts of the Jersey public at the time, but even so it does not seem very likely, a possible explanation being that as the saddle tank *General Don* had been lying idle from December 1877 until 1883 the name plates were removed and transferred to the standard gauge engine.

A fortnight after the trial trip from St. Aubin to La Moye two narrow-gauge tank engines arrived from Manning, Wardle & Company, of Leeds, namely No. 1, *St. Heliers* and No. 2, *St. Aubyns*. They were of the 2-4-0^T type, with coupled wheels 3 ft. 6 ins. in diameter, cylinders 13 in. x 18 in., boiler diameter 3 ft. 1 in., heating surface 560 square feet, working pressure 140 lb. and weight in working order 25 tons. To begin with they were employed exclusively between St. Aubin and Bel Royal and later, when the gauge conversion was complete, between St. Helier and St. Aubin. Through working between St. Helier and Corbiere (La Moye) did not become possible until August, 1885, and it is evident that the saddle tanks were solely responsible until then for the Corbiere extension, after which *St. Heliers* and *St. Aubyns* normally ran St. Helier—St. Aubin—Corbiere, but were helped out by the saddle tanks at times of particularly heavy traffic or when either was undergoing repair.

Locomotive No. 3 *Corbiere* was delivered by W. G. Bagnall Limited of Stafford in July 1893 and had a tractive force of 8,850 lb. There were slight differences as compared with the earlier pair, the boiler diameter being 3 ft. 2¾ ins., cylinders 13 in. x 20 in., heating surface 572 square feet, working pressure 135 lb. and weight in working order 23 tons. In addition, the newcomer had a smokebox that was "waisted" near the bottom whereas, in the case of Nos. 1 and 2, the sides went straight up and down. The two last-named had a circular window in each side sheet of the cab. All three had outside frames and compensating levers between the coupled wheels.

This was the sum total of the locomotive stock until after the formation of the Jersey Railways & Tramways Limited, in January 1896. As, however, No. 4 *St. Brelades* arrived in the Island less than a fortnight after this event it is obvious that it had been ordered by the old régime. It was exactly similar to No. 3 and was by the same builders. The four 2-4-0's were fully capable of handling all the traffic offering, and it must be assumed that the saddle tanks were withdrawn from service. In fact, it is doubtful whether they were used much after the introduction of *Corbiere*.

Between 1907 and 1912 all four engines were rebuilt with boilers of 3 ft. 6¼ ins. diameter and with Ramsbottom safety valves on the firebox in place of the original spring balance valves on the dome. The total heating surface was increased to 635 square feet, the diameter of the cylinders to 13⅜ ins. and the weight to 26 tons. Engine No. 3 was dealt with in 1907, No. 2 in 1909, No. 1 in 1910 and No. 4 in 1912.

As already mentioned, electrification of the system was seriously considered in 1906, but presumably the cost of conversion and of new equipment was found to be out of all proportion to the estimated saving in running expenses and the likely increase in traffic. Instead, a new locomotive was ordered, a 2-4-0T considerably more powerful than its four predecessors. No. 5 *La Moye* was built by Andrew Barclay & Company. The diameter of the leading and coupled wheels was the same as before, but Walschaerts valve gear was fitted instead of Stephenson's link motion. Cylinders were 15½ in. x 22 in., heating surface 792 square feet, grate area 12 square feet, working pressure 185 lb. and weight in working order 36½ tons.

Unfortunately No. 5 was found to be very heavy on the track, particularly on the sharply-curved sections beyond St. Aubin, and one cannot help wondering whether, in the long run, the 8-wheeled engine originally suggested, with a slightly greater total weight distributed over four axles, would not have been preferable to one with only three. *La Moye* was also a heavy coal burner and in consequence was seldom used after July 1914.

In January 1921 the general report by a Great Western Railway engineer stated that as the permanent way was being strengthened No. 5 was likely to be of great service. For some time past the board had been thinking of selling the engine, but now decided first to enquire of the makers the cost of a new copper firebox and set of brass tubes and received a quotation for £700. It was considered that this was too high to be economical, and efforts were made to effect a sale. An enquiry was received about a year later, when the price asked was £1,000. In August 1924 the manager wrote to the Constable of St. Helier, saying that he understood a new boiler would soon be required at the destructor and offered the boiler for No. 5 for £150. Fortunately, as things turned out, this offer was not accepted. Finally, in 1928, the engine was sold as it stood for £550 to the Victoria Falls Power Company.

A few notes on the methods of engine working in the days before the introduction of the railcars may be of interest. A three-week roster was in operation, with an early and late turn, and on Sundays there were always two engines in steam. If No. 1 engine were on duty on

Sunday it worked with its own driver turn No. 1, which ended at 4-42 p.m. No. 4 would take the late turn, beginning at 2 o'clock and finishing at 10-15 p.m. The next day, No. 3 would work both early and late turns, No. 4 on Tuesday, No. 1 on Wednesday, No. 3 on Thursday, No. 4 on Friday and No. 1 on Saturday. On the second Sunday No. 3 would be early and No. 1 late; then Nos. 4, 1, 3, 4, 1 and 3 until the third Sunday, when No. 4 would be early, No. 3 late, and Nos. 1, 3, 4, 1, 3 and 4 completed the week. On the fourth Sunday No. 1 would be early, No. 4 late, and the cycle was repeated. Engine No. 2 was normally the spare, and on race days and other occasions of heavy traffic was used as a banking engine from St. Aubin to Don Bridge.

An uncommon feature of the J. R. & T. locomotives was the provision of acetylene headlights, the generating plant being carried on the footplate near the sidetank. It is believed that these headlights were introduced about 1907 when clerestory carriage No. 11 was fitted with acetylene lighting. Engine No. 4 had a bell whistle; the others had "Caledonian" hooters. All engines carried a jack.

Latterly the engines were painted olive green, lined in yellow, black and vermilion, the buffer beams being vermilion. Formerly, they were painted a dark shade of green, with broad white lining. Nos. 1 to 4 had brass tops to the chimneys, brass number plates on the front of the chimneys and on the back of the cabs; in addition they had brass name plates with raised letters on a vermilion background. All four were scrapped in Jersey in 1937, but thanks to the efforts of Mr. V. Boyd-Carpenter the name and number plates were presented to the Railway Museum at York. Engine No. 5 had a plain chimney and the name and number were painted on the side tanks in gilt letters.

Sentinel Rail Cars

The railcars have been described in detail in the text, and it remains to mention here that Nos. 1, 2 and 3 were originally painted yellow, as were the light four-wheel trailers used at times of heavy pressure between St. Helier and St. Aubin. When purchased from the Jersey Eastern Railway *Normandy* was red and it is believed that this colour was retained for a few months, but that in 1931 all four were painted green and cream to conform with the colour scheme of the Jersey Motor Transport buses. All four railcars were fitted with letter boxes.

It was decided at a board meeting held on 17 June 1935 to dispose of the body of No. 1 railcar, and as No. 1 was not included in the equipment sold in 1937, it seems that it had already been sold or scrapped. The motive units of the other three Sentinels were used in the dismantling of the line, and at the conclusion of these duties they were scrapped.

Carriages (Standard Gauge)

The passenger carriages used when the line was opened in 1870 were of two distinct kinds—open and closed four-wheelers. The closed carriages, intended for winter use, were built in England and arrived by the same steamer as the two pioneer locomotives.

The open carriages were built by the company and some of them had outside verandahs along each side, giving them a total width of no less than 13 ft. 9 ins. An engineer, writing to the *British Press & Jersey Times* in November 1870, suggested that the hinged brass bar provided for each doorway should be removed as it was too high to prevent children from falling out, was often left unfastened and passengers joining the trains at intermediate stations usually ducked underneath or entered the carriages at the extreme ends. Instead, he advocated a light wooden door on hinges. Nothing was done for six years when, in October 1876, it was announced that the verandahs were on the point of being removed in order to decrease wind resistance and oscillation and permit an increase in speed.

On 18 July 1884, with the aid of horses, the company transferred several closed carriages to the Jersey Eastern Railway. "This difficult operation, bearing in mind the length of the carriages, was made via Mulcaster Street, Hill Street and Green Street." The number of carriages purchased is believed to have been four. Some or all of the open carriages were retained until September 1884, when the change of gauge was completed. They were used subsequently for such purposes as platelayers' huts.

Carriages (Narrow Gauge)

The first 3 ft. 6 ins. gauge passenger train in Jersey ran from St. Aubin to La Moye and back on 15 March 1884. It is not known what carriage (or carriages) were used on that occasion, but it was announced a fortnight later that 10 carriages and three brake vans were on order. As likely as not one or more of these had already arrived and were used at the trial. In any event, these early carriages were what became known as "long" carriages, with seats along the sides as in an old-fashioned omnibus or tram, the two rows of passengers facing each other. In July 1887, the Bristol Wagon Works Company supplied four new carriages of the ordinary compartment type.

Two carriages were ordered from the Ashbury Railway Carriage & Ironworks Company in 1896, but the order was postponed owing to the possibility of the introduction of electric traction. It was reinstated in July 1897. It is almost certain that these two carriages ran on four-wheel bogies, and probable that this applied also to most, if not all, of the earlier narrow gauge carriages apart from the four-wheeled brake vans. The annual report for 1899 showed that the company owned 21 carriages and 16 wagons, the carriage stock being increased by one in the following year.

The earliest written mention of the use of bogie carriages seems to have been in connection with a collision at First Tower in September 1902, the company's minute book stating that two wheels of one of the bogies of carriage No. 7 were derailed. In 1907 a bogie carriage with clerestory roof, lighted by acetylene gas and capable of seating 50 passengers, was built in the company's works and became No. 11. At about the same time the ends of some of the "long" carriages were enclosed and carriages Nos. 3 and 5 were extensively rebuilt. It was decided to build four new steel bogies. It was mentioned at the annual general meeting in 1910 that the last of an obsolete pattern of bogies would be superseded by four more bogies then under construction. By the end of 1913 all carriages were lighted by electricity and three, brake vans were fitted with dynamos and accumulators.

Latterly the company possessed 23 carriages and brake vans, an interesting feature being that three brake vans were fitted with letter boxes. There were only two classes—first and second. At one time all passenger rolling stock was painted green with yellow and black lettering, but latterly five carriages were finished in what was known in railways circles as "varnished teak".

Mention has already been made of the fitting of vacuum brakes to the passenger rolling stock in 1903-04, and of the fact that the use of this brake was soon discontinued.

Train Sets

Before the days of the railcars there were normally two train sets in use, a third being in reserve, and, like the locomotives, they worked early or late turns. Each set comprised a four-wheel brake, a "long" second bogie, and two first and second bogie composites. One of the last-mentioned had a large first class compartment with seating on a horseshoe plan and this had been made by knocking two second class compartments into one. Except possibly when the vacuum brake was in use, all trains between St. Aubin and Corbiere had a brake van at the St. Helier end in case of a breakaway during the steep climb out of St. Aubin.

Other coaches were added to the sets for special purposes—for example, a four-wheel brake second (with two compartments) was often attached around noon for carrying prams and was usually detached about 6 p.m., being always stabled at St. Helier.

For many years the 7-30 a.m. from St. Helier to Corbiere stopped outside St. Aubin for the leading coach to be detached and left in No. 1 platform, thus avoiding any likelihood of the train stalling on the bank. The return train—that is to say, the 8-6 a.m. from Corbiere— ran through Corbiere platform No. 3 at St. Aubin and was backed into No. 1 to pick up the coach that had been left there and also, in term time, the coach for the boys of Victoria College, which was always left by the buffer stops on platform 1. The College coach returned from St. Helier by the 9-5 a.m. and was picked up again at 3-30 p.m. by the train from Corbiere, which ran through platform 3 and backed into No. 1. It finally returned on the 4-5 p.m. from St. Helier. On Saturdays, however, the coach was used all day to strengthen the trains.

Goods Traffic

It will be recalled that the original title of the railway extension from St. Aubin to Corbiere was the St. Aubin's & La Moye Railway & Granite Quarries Company Limited. When the Jersey Railways Company Limited was formed in 1884 and undertook to complete the line an arrangement was apparently made with the then owner of the quarries, Mr. T. Hayward Budd, to guarantee a minimum freight revenue of £2,000 a year for three years, equivalent to a movement of 75,000 tons of granite a year over the railway. The writer has had access to the revenue figures of the J.R. and J. R. & T. from 1884 to 1936, and the goods takings make rather sad reading. Nothing at all was shown for 1884 or 1885, but in 1886 sums of exactly £3,000 and £1,500 were received and in 1887 £1,668. It looks, therefore, as if a total of £6,168 was received by the railway for the years 1885-87, and as it can be assumed that there was some goods traffic other than granite it would seem that Mr. Budd was called upon to honour his guarantee. As through running between St. Helier and La Moye was not possible before 5 August 1885 one would expect the penalty clause to have applied only from that date.

The goods takings in 1888 were £1,836, after which they slumped badly and for the years 1889 to 1933 inclusive they only averaged £278 a year. And even this figure was boosted appreciably by the fact that the takings in 1897-98, the first two years of the J. R. & T., averaged over £500 a year and from 1921-25 inclusive nearly £600 a year, the increase in the latter case being due largely to sand and gravel traffic from some new quarries near La Moye station.

The J. R. & T. annual report for 1897 announced the purchase of the quarries and lands belonging to the heirs of the late Mr. T. Hayward Budd at La Moye and elsewhere, the sum paid being £2,218 less £608 owing to the company. At a board meeting in July 1899, it was resolved that as Mr. Green, the contractor for St. Aubin's tunnel and Corbiere station, had purchased the La Moye quarries from the company, the existing rates for the carriage of stone, gravel, etc., namely 6/- a truck for dressed stone or rubble and 5/- a truck for cracked stone, gravel and quarry rubbish, would not be increased during Mr. Green's ownership of the quarries, with the reservation that these rates would apply only to trucks of the size then in use.

In 1899-1900 the company owned 16 wagons, and at one time the number was as high as 21. Latterly very few remained.

During the years 1885-88 there must have been many special goods trains to cope with the granite traffic. Latterly, there was only one "mixed" train each way a week. On Fridays, the 3-35 p.m. passenger train from Corbiere stopped at the junction, where the engine was detached and proceeded to the quarry to collect the loaded wagons, which were then attached to the front of the train and the journey was resumed. On the following Monday or Tuesday the empty wagons would be attached to the front of the afternoon train to Corbiere, which would stop at the junction. The engine would then proceed with them to the old Corbiere station, run around them, push them to the quarry and then rejoin the train.

An unusual accident ocurred in the 1890's. It seems that an engine was standing on the quarry side of a rake of wagons in the La Moye Quarry siding and that its crew had left the footplate without applying the brakes. As customary, two of the wagons had brakes mounted on an end platform but the others were without brakes. Owing to the fact that one of these brake wagons had not had its brakes applied, the rake began to move, pushing the engine to the end of the rails and into the quarry, whence it was eventually rescued.

Signals

There was no signalling in the accepted sense, and the only tele-
phone communication between the stations was by the normal
States service. There was, however, one semaphore signal on the
western side of St. Aubin's tunnel, interconnected with the gates of
the level crossing opposite St. Aubin's Post Office. The signal showed
clear when these gates were open to the trains and went to danger when
they were closed.

With few exceptions the level crossings had swing gates, generally
similar in pattern to those used in the United Kingdom. Rising poles
were fitted at the level crossing to the east of Don Bridge station in
accordance with the board's resolution of 21 August 1911, the gen-
erally-familiar continental pattern being adopted.

Permanent Way

Flat-bottomed rails were dogged direct to the sleepers.
From September 1909 onwards rails weighing 70 lb. a yard were used
for renewals, and from 1925 onwards 75 lb. became the new standard.

Gradients

A survey of the line beyond St. Aubin was prepared jointly by
the Company and Sentinel-Cammell prior to the tests of rail car No.
2 in January 1924. Readings started at the eastern end of St. Aubin's
tunnel and showed a gradient of 1 in 30 for 200 feet, 1 in 31 for 200
feet, 1 in 32 for 200 feet, 1 in 33 for 200 feet and 1 in 35 for 200 feet—
with an average of 1 in 32 for the total distance of 1,000 feet. Over the
1.4 miles from the tunnel entrance to Don Bridge station the average
gradient was 1 in 40.

The summit level was about a quarter of a mile beyond Don
Bridge, the rise from the tunnel to that point being 211 feet. Onwards
to Corbiere the line fell at an average gradient of 1 in 140.

The short length of 1 in 30 was, of course, of very great severity
and was exactly similar in steepness to the much longer stretch on the

Folkestone Harbour branch of British Railways. As far as can be ascertained there are only two steeper stretches (both 1 in 27) tackled by passenger trains in the British Isles.

Stations

When the line was opened in 1870 the termini at St. Helier and St. Aubin had roofs similar in design and construction. That at St. Aubin was replaced in 1922 on safety grounds.

The St. Helier roof was replaced shortly before the construction of the office building in 1901. From then onwards there was one island platform with two sets of rails on either side. On the road (or north) side the outer line represented the run-around loop and from 1902 onwards was also connected with the inner line by a traverser. The outer line on the sea side was a siding.

The platform was lengthened by 50 feet in 1913.

St. Aubin's station, as originally built, had two platforms, that on the road (or west) side, No. 1, being in regular use—hence the crossover to enable the incoming engine to run round the train. When through running between St. Helier and Corbiere started in 1885 an additional platform (No. 3) was opened for the Corbiere trains.

The new Millbrook station, opened in 1912, had two platforms and two running lines as had the old station it replaced. The platform on the north side was used by both up and down trains except when two were due to cross, in which case it was used by the up train. There was a crossing loop at Don Bridge, but only a single platform on the north side of the through line. At the new Corbiere terminus there was a single platform on the south side of the line, and a loop for the engine to run round the train. The remainder of the line was single and the stations had single platforms, but there were sidings on the country side of First Tower station and on the town side of Millbrook, opened in 1911 and 1912 respectively. A short branch left the main line opposite Castle Street, St. Helier, and led to the commencement of the Albert Pier. After World War I a short siding beyond La Moye station served a gravel quarry.

The original station at Corbiere (La Moye Quarries) was closed when the new extension and station were opened in 1899, but the line continued to serve the quarries. Shortly afterwards a "halt" was built on the town side of Corbiere junction and was used mainly by workers at the quarries although apparently the general public were set down or picked up as and when required. The station bore no name board but was known locally as "The Temporary".

Speed

Mention has already been made that during one of the trials prior to the official opening of the line in 1870 a standard-gauge train was reported to have travelled non-stop from St. Helier to St. Aubin in seven minutes. Assuming that the duration of the run was correctly recorded and assessing the distance at 3¾ miles the average speed was 32 m.p.h. As the train was not fitted with continuous brakes the driver would have been obliged to slow down some considerable distance before St. Aubin, and this suggests that the maximum speed attained must have been in the region of 45 m.p.h.—probably quite a hair-raising experience for passengers travelling in four-wheeled carriages on a lightly-ballasted track! The return journey was stated to have been completed in 7½ minutes.

On an occasion in 1918 a friend of the writer travelled from St. Aubin to St. Helier in a train that stopped at all stations except La Haule and completed the journey in the remarkable time of 11½ minutes. That is to say, the average speed inclusive of five stops was 20 m.p.h. The engine was No. 2 *St. Aubyns*, the driver Fitzgerald and the whole of the front of the engine was red hot by the time it reached its destination.

One of the few contemporary newspaper references to speed appeared on the occasion of the first trial trip of *The Pioneer No. 1*, in 1923, when it was stated that 35 m.p.h. was attained during part of the journey.

During the 1930's another friend of the writer deliberately kept pace in his car with a stopping train between First Tower and West Park and for some distance his speedometer remained constant at 30 m.p.h. It is probable that this was about the maximum speed attained by stopping trains between St. Helier and St. Aubin and about the normal maximum for the railcars, but non-stop locomotive-hauled trains often attained at least 35 m.p.h.

It is believed that the record non-stop journey time from St. Helier to Corbiere (7¾ miles) was 16 minutes and that driver Fitzgerald, who had quite a reputation as a "Jehu", was the one responsible. Bearing in mind the succession of sharp curves beyond St. Aubin and the 1½ miles of gradient averaging 1 in 40 an average speed of 29 m.p.h. must have been quite a thrilling experience.

Information has been received from two or three people that the brakes of railcar No. 2 were a constant source of anxiety to the driver on the steep descent from Don Bridge to St. Aubin and it seems that the manager refused to sanction the comparatively small cost of fitting steam brakes in spite of the fact that the locomotive superintendent was strongly in favour of this being done. The hand brakes were not powerful enough for an emergency and it was an accepted practice to place the engine in reverse. On a certain occasion early in 1929 the hand throttle would not close fully and a rather more vigorous reversal than usual resulted in one of the cylinders being cracked. In fact, this may well have been done deliberately in order to draw attention to a dangerous state of affairs.

Accidents

The Jersey Railway and its successors remained singularly free from serious accidents in the 66 years they were open to traffic. In fact, no trace has been found of any passenger or railway servant suffering any serious injury as the result of an accident to the train in which he or she was travelling, and the cases of slight injury were very few indeed. Unfortunately, several people committed suicide on the railway—usually by placing their heads on the rails when a train was approaching. One or two people were knocked down when crossing the line and either killed or seriously injured. Two passengers were killed—one, a lady, in attempting to board a moving train at First Tower, and a man who alighted in the dark from the wrong side of a carriage at St. Helier, fell upon the permanent way and shortly afterwards was run over by the engine, which was running round the train.

One or two accidents merit description, and in particular the collision during the early hours of 6 September 1902, when locomotive No. 1, running light, ran into the rear of a special train from St. Aubin's to St. Helier as it was leaving First Tower, after stopping there to set down passengers. The brake van (No. 17) was derailed, both buffer beams smashed and one pane of glass cracked; No. 7 carriage had two wheels of a bogie derailed, one buffer beam broken and 10 panes of 21 ounce sheet glass shattered. After an exhaustive enquiry the board reprimanded the guard for not having the red tail light in the proper position. (It had been left at the other end of the train.) It was extremely fortunate that at the time of the collision the train was on the move. Had it been stationary in First Tower station with the brakes on the results would undoubtedly have been very serious.

A derailment at Greenville on 18 July 1893 might also have been serious. The driver was proceeding cautiously at the time and immediately the engine went off the line he reversed it and applied the steam brake. It proceeded for some 20 yards, and finished up near the edge of a 30 foot unprotected embankment. A telegram was sent to St. Helier from St. Aubin and Mr. Dickson, the manager, proceeded with Mr. A. Curry, the engineer and all available staff to the scene of the accident on locomotive No. 3, which had arrived in the Island a few days previously. On reaching Greenville, the plug was removed from the bottom of the water tank of No. 1 so as to empty this and relieve the overhanging weight. By means of a jack and wedges the engine was lifted into a horizontal position. Work was continued until 11 p.m. and shortly after being resumed the following morning the engine was got back on the track. The line remained out of commission for the remainder of the day whilst the permanent way was being repaired. A similar accident occurred within a short distance of the same spot in January 1897.

A collision at Corbiere on Whit Sunday, 13 May 1913, occurred at a time when trains were being run in duplicate. At 6 p.m. a train drawn by locomotive No. 3 and full of passengers was apparently being shunted into the siding when an empty train, drawn by No. 2, put in an appearance. Upon approaching the station the brakes failed to grip and the driver whistled for the guard and brakesman to apply their brakes. Even so the train collided with the full one, the buffers of whose front brake van jumped those of the adjacent long second class carriage and smashed the wooden protecting rails to the platform. The van was lifted by means of a jack, and the train was recoupled and left for St. Helier only 10 minutes late. One passenger had a few bruises. At a subsequent enquiry it was decided that the driver was approaching Corbiere too fast and he was reprimanded. It is clear that the use of the vacuum brake had been discontinued by this time; it is unlikely that the accident would have happened had it been in operation.

The chairman took a grave view of the mishap on 10 February 1920 concerning three wagons containing sand which got out of control when proceeding by gravity from Pont Marquet to St. Aubin. In spite of the efforts of three men operating the brake handles and two men sanding the rails to try and make the brakes grip the wagons smashed through three gates and came to a standstill opposite the water crane at the end of No. 3 platform in St. Aubin's station. The chairman explained that movement by gravity was not admitted by the law and that the company would have been liable for any injuries to the public. It was decided that in future no ballasting was to be done without an engine being in attendance and attached to the trucks.

Conclusion

There are many people who believe that if the J. R. & T. were in existence today with its original rolling stock and permanent way it could at least be made to pay during the summer months, and in view of the tremendous increase in the number of visitors to Jersey in comparison with pre-war days this might well be the case, particularly if a Preservation Society were formed to run it on a partly voluntary basis as with the Festiniog and Talyllyn Railways in Wales. However, it is of no use speculating as there is no prospect whatever of any revival. The most that enthusiasts can hope for is to be allowed to see the magnificent scale working model of the J. R. & T. built and owned by Mr. M. Deane of Backwell, Somerset, through whose courtesy a photograph is reproduced.

Appendix A

LOCOMOTIVES

JERSEY RAILWAY, ST. AUBIN'S & LA MOYE RAILWAY, JERSEY RAILWAYS, JERSEY RAILWAYS & TRAMWAYS

Standard Gauge (4 ft. 8½ ins.)

Date built	Works Nos.	Jersey Nos.	Names	Wheel Armt.	Builders	See Note
1870	2047	1	HARO HARO	2-4-0 T	Sharp Stewart	A
1870	2048	2	DUKE OF NORMANDY	2-4-0 T	Sharp Stewart	B
1871	2140	3	————	2-4-0 T	Sharp Stewart	
1871–2	2241	?	NORTH WESTERN	2-4-0 T	Sharp Stewart	C
1878–9	1222	?	GENERAL DON	2-4-0 T	Dubs	D

Narrow Gauge (3 ft 6 ins.)

Date built	Works Nos.	Jersey Nos.	Names	Wheel Armt.	Builders	See Note
1877	?	4(?)	GENERAL DON	0-4-2 ST(?)	Black Hawthorn (?)	E
1877	?	5(?)	?	0-4-2 ST(?)	Black Hawthorn (?)	E
1884	916	1	ST. HELIERS	2-4-0 T	Manning Wardle	F
1884	917	2	ST. AUBYNS	2-4-0 T	Manning Wardle	F
1893	1418	3	CORBIERE	2-4-0 T	Bagnall	F
1896	1466	4	ST. BRELADES	2-4-0 T	Bagnall	F
1907	1105	5	LA MOYE	2-4-0 T	Andrew Barclay	G
1923	—	Rail Car 1	THE PIONEER No. 1	Railcar	Sentinel-Cammell	H
1924	—	,, 2	THE PIONEER No. 2*	Railcar	Sentinel-Cammell	F
1925 (acquired)	—	,, 3	LA MOYE	Railcar	Sentinel-Cammell	F
1930　,,	—	,, 4	NORMANDY	Railcar	Sentinel-Cammell	FI

NOTES: A. Later worked on construction of Manchester Ship canal.　B. Later worked on construction of Manchester Ship Canal; subsequently sold to T. W. Ward of Sheffield. 1897 resold to Vulcan Foundry. Scrapped 1904.　C. 1878 sold to Jersey Eastern Railway.　D. Later became CLEVEDON of Weston, Clevedon & Portishead Railway. Scrapped 1940.　E. Re-shipped from Jersey 1899-1900 (?).　F. Scrapped 1937.　G. Sold 1928 to Victoria Falls Power Co.　H. Withdrawn 1935. I. Built 1927 for Jersey Eastern Railway, from whom purchased; converted from standard gauge. *Later renamed PORTELET.

Appendix B

STATIONS

Distance		Opened	Closed
0.0	St. Helier (St. Helier's)	25/10/1870	——
0.4	Cheapside	14/ 2/1872	
	renamed Westmount		
	renamed West Park	2/1896	——
	People's Park	14/ 2/1872	20/ 7/1872
	Bellozanne Halt	5/1923	——
1.1	First Tower	25/10/1870	——
	Millbrook Halt	1923	——
1.6	Millbrook (Old Station)	25/10/1870	14/ 1/1912
	Millbrook (New Station)	15/ 1/1912	——
2.1	Bel Royal (Old Station)	1/11/1872	1920
	Bel Royal (New Station)	1920	——
	Bel Royal Halt	1923	——
2.6	Beaumont	25/10/1870	——
	Beaumont Halt	1923	——
3.1	La Haule	1876 or earlier	——
3.75	St. Aubin (St. Aubin's)	25/10/1870	——
	St. Aubin's (temporary station near St. Aubin's hospital)	30/ 8/1884	4/ 8/1885
4.6	Greenville	30/ 8/1884	30/ 6/1899
4.9	Pont Marquet	?	——
5.3	Don Bridge (Don's Bridge)	30/ 8/1884	——
6.2	Blanches Banques	?	——
6.6	La Moye (La Moie)	30/ 8/1884	——
7.1	"The Temporary"	about 1899	——
7.3	Corbiere (La Moye Quarries)	30/ 8/1884	30/ 6/1899
7.6	Corbiere	1/ 7/1899	——

Unless otherwise stated, all stations were closed on 30/9/1936 and were never re-opened.

Names in brackets are alternative spellings.

"The Temporary" was constructed immediately on the town side of Corbiere junction and was used mainly by workers at the La Moye Quarries after the closure of the original Corbiere station.

Appendix C

JERSEY RAILWAYS COMPANY, LIMITED

REVENUE

Year	1885	1886	1887	1888	1889	1890	1891	1892	1893	1894	1895
	£	£	£	£	£	£	£	£	£	£	£
Passengers											
First class	684	610	582	645	594	614	619	670	570	598	639
Second class	5,035	4,700	4,809	4,852	4,816	4,813	5,304	5,707	5,669	6,120	6,728
Season tickets	504	426	436	443	411	393	365	376	356	421	566
	6,223	5,736	5,827	5,940	5,821	5,820	6,288	6,753	6,595	7,139	7,933
Parcels	103	135	161	178	189	194	219	237	234	222	256
Goods	nil	4,500	1,668	1,836	390	306	52	1	135	303	484
Miscellaneous	375	315	349	353	289	276	330	402	551	665	590
TOTAL	6,701	10,686	8,005	8,307	6,689	6,596	6,889	7,393	7,515	8,329	9,263

Appendix D JERSEY RAILWAYS & TRAMWAYS LIMITED

REVENUE

Year	1925 £	1926 £	1927 £	1928 £	1929 £	1930 £	1931 £	1932 £	1933 £	1934 £	1935 £	1936 £
Passengers												
First class	1,391	1,004	867	578	363	362	25	16	3	12	14	16
Second class	18,962	16,700	16,271	16,018	16,635	15,069	14,524	4,525	3,617	3,063	3,015	3,069
Season tickets	894	804	847	838	802	562	488	418	142	98	108	104
	21,247	18,508	17,985	17,434	17,800	15,993	15,037	5,059	3,762	3,173	3,137	3,189
Parcels	1,017	916	848	695	631	541	401	323	174	117	79	74
Goods	471	340	338	152	383	141	68	74	3	nil	nil	nil
Miscellaneous	740	639	612	1,099	794	541	326	2,204	2,181	2,208	5,009	5,170
Total	23,475	20,403	19,783	19,380	19,608	17,216	15,832	7,660	6,120	5,498	8,225	8,433
Working expenses	21,009	18,647	17,529	17,843	18,100	17,101	16,419	8,945	6,357	5,919	7,272	7,450
Profit or loss	+2466	+1756	+2254	+1537	+1508	+115	−587	−1285	−237	−421	+953	+983

NOTES: 1925 was the most successful year in the Company's history.
1932-33-34 each include under Miscellaneous a hire charge of £2,000 from the Jersey Motor Transport in respect of the J.R. & T. buses.
1935 and 1936. Miscellaneous includes sums of £1,700 and £2,100 respectively received from the J.M.T. in respect of interchangeable tickets. And in addition substantial dividends from them.
From October 1931 onwards the St. Aubin—Corbiere section was closed between October and April inclusive.
The entire railway was closed from 1 December 1932 to 30 April 1933; and in subsequent winters between October and April inclusive.

JERSEY RAILWAYS & TRAMWAYS LIMITED

Year	No. of Passengers	Gross Receipts £	Ordinary Dividend (per cent)
1896		8,499 *	3
1897		9,736	3
1898		9,534	3
1899		9,094	2½
1900		8,594	2
1901		8,717	2
1902	604,591	9,122	2
1903	628,232	9,797	2
1904	630,736	10,028	2
1905	593,234	9,306	2
1906	613,375	9,792	2
1907	607,476	9,852	2
1908	635,332	10,211	2
1909	657,518	10,643	2½
1910	675,163	10,751	3
1911	695,382	11,115	3
1912	660,060	10,891	3
1913	726,390	11,704	4
1914	617,990	9,840	3
1915	558,521	9,035	3
1916	513,149	8,258	nil
1917	488,854	8,391	nil
1918	521,669	9,275	nil
1919	711,235	14,406	4
1920	814,638	21,834	4
1921	824,082	22,506	5
1922	871,294	23,637	6
1923	862,510	21,940	6
1924	1,000,607	21,126	6
1925	1,091,789	23,475	7
1926	999,667	20,403	5
1927	949,428	19,783	5
1928	970,986	19,380	6
1929		19,608	6
1930		17,216	nil
1931		15,832	nil
1932		7,661 **	1½
1933		6,120 **	nil
1934		5,498 **	nil
1935		5,194	2½
1936		5,607	2½

Note: No. of passengers carried was exclusive of season ticket holders.   *–For 11 months.
**–Includes £2,000 from Jersey Motor Transport Co. Ltd. for hire of J. R. & T. buses.

Appendix F

GLOSSARY OF JERSEY NAMES AND TERMS

LIEUTENANT-GOVERNOR	The representative of the Crown.
BAILIFF	Chief Magistrate and President of the States of Jersey.
GREFFIER	Registrar of the States.
VISCOUNT	The office of Viscount combines the duties of Sheriff and Coroner.

AU GREFFE	Bills lodged "au Greffe" are printed and distributed to members of the States for further consideration at a later date.
CLAMEUR DE HARO	An article in the *British Press & Jersey Times* of 7 June 1870 described the "Clameur de Haro" as a "Norman relic of the barbarous old feudal times". It may be raised by anyone upon whose land a trespass occurs. The accuser must fall on one knee and in the presence of witnesses cry: "Haro! Haro! A l'aide, mon Prince. On me fait tort". (Haro! Haro! Help, my Prince. I have been wronged.) The offender must immediately withdraw and the case is then taken to the Royal Court. The accuser is liable to a heavy fine if the "Clameur" is raised without adequate justification, and in this connection it should be pointed out that Article 55 of the Jersey Railway Bill specifically forbade the raising of the "Clameur" and that the trespass complained of by Jurat De Quetteville did not take place on his own land.
DÉCRET	Decree (of bankruptcy).
DÉSASTRE	Bankruptcy.
TENANT APRÈS DÉCRET	Tenant of the property after the bankruptcy decree.

(ST.) HELIER	Pronounced Hell-yer.	
(ST.) AUBIN	„	O-bin.
(ST.) BRELADE	„	Brell-ard.

ADDENDA AND CORRIGENDA

(1969 reprint)

P. 17. (last paragraph). This turntable was at St. Aubin, on the spot later occupied by the carriage shed and was no doubt removed when the change of gauge took place. It is known that at least one of the engines had a turnround, and the carriages probably had a periodic one also as the paintwork on the side facing the sea would have received much more wear than that on the land side.

P. 59 The mystery of the missing locomotive is explained by the fact that a Jersey Railway locomotive—undoubtedly No. 2140—was shipped from Jersey on 11 May 1872 per ss MINERVA to Tunis for Mr. Pickering's Tunis Railway Company. This locomotive was replaced by No. 2241, which was named NORTH WESTERN.

P. 65 (last paragraph). According to "Locomotives and Railways", published for a short time during the very early years of the present century, the locomotives were then painted chocolate. It is believed that they were painted green from the time of the introduction of LA MOYE in 1907.

P. 67 (penultimate paragraph). It is quite certain that the two carriages ordered from the Ashbury Railway Carriage & Ironworks Company in 1897 ran on four-wheel bogies, as did the "long" carriages of 1884 and the compartment-type carriages of 1884 and the compartment-type carriages of 1887.

P. 68 (second paragraph). According to "Locomotives and Railways", the carriages were then varnished. At a later date, perhaps from 1907 when the engine colours were changed, they were painted red with yellow and black lettering. Lattterly, five carriages were finished in what was known in railway circles as "varnished teak."

P. 70 (last paragraph). The Jersey "Evening Post" of 18 May 1895 gave the following account of what happened on the previous day:—
"Alarming incident to No. 1 engine at Corbiere terminus of Jersey Railways Company. Quite recently the track has been extended beyond the Corbiere terminus and continued over the brow of the hill, right down to the quarry—an incline of 1 in 4. This was done to enable trucks to collect stone in the quarry and then be hauled up by a stout cable attached to the engine at the top of the hill. However, on this occasion the engine was as usual pushing the trucks over the top of the hill so as to let them run down of their own accord, but as the signal was given the engine failed to break and the whole lot was precipitated to the bottom of the quarry. All three engines will to-morrow go to Corbiere to drag No. 1 out. The event is unfortunate as the Company is fixing a stationary engine at the top of the hill to eliminate this sort of thing. The engine, although keeping to the line, was damaged and the men, standing on the trucks to apply the brakes, all jumped clear. Several trucks were telescoped and smashed, after terrific speed."

(Note. The author is grateful to Messrs. G. E. Baddeley, K. Benest, Robin Cox and Michael Ginns for much of the above information.)

INDEX